DATE DUE

MAY 07 2013	
AUG 26 2013	
JAN 13 2014	
APR 03 2014	

READING CORMAC McCARTHY

READING CORMAC McCARTHY

Willard P. Greenwood

The Pop Lit Book Club

GREENWOOD PRESS
An Imprint of ABC-CLIO, LLC

A B C 🔖 C L I O

Santa Barbara, California • Denver, Colorado • Oxford, England

Copyright 2009 by Willard P. Greenwood

Library of Congress Cataloging-in-Publication Data

Greenwood, Willard P.
  Reading Cormac McCarthy / Willard P. Greenwood.
    p.   cm. — (The Pop Lit Book Club)
  Includes bibliographical references and index.
  ISBN 978-0-313-35664-3 (hard copy : alk. paper) —
ISBN 978-0-313-35665-0 (ebook)
    1. McCarthy, Cormac, 1933–   —Criticism and interpretation.
2. Mexican-American Border Region—In literature. 3. Southern
States—In literature. I. Title.
PS3563.C337Z665   2009
813'.54—dc22   2009010178

13   12   11   10   09   1   2   3   4   5

This book is also available on the World Wide Web as an eBook.
Visit www.abc-clio.com for details.

ABC-CLIO, LLC
130 Cremona Drive, P.O. Box 1911
Santa Barbara, California 93116-1911

This book is printed on acid-free paper ∞

Manufactured in the United States of America

CONTENTS

PREFACE

The first time I heard of Cormac McCarthy was in 1994. I was in Atlanta, Georgia, on the verge of starting classes for a master's degree in English at Georgia State University. I was sitting in the apartment of my friend and mentor Austin Hummell. Austin and I had met as students at the University of Maine—I was an undergraduate, he was earning a master's degree in English. Our paths diverged for several years, until I asked Austin to write me a recommendation. I was granted conditional enrollment. Describing my undergraduate performance, Austin wrote something to the effect of—like all poets my grades were "uneven."

Soon after I got to Atlanta, Austin had organized a writers' conference at which Jorie Graham was one of the speakers. This was just before Graham won the Pulitzer Prize. In between conference events, I was at Austin's apartment with Graham. During our talk, she pulled out a copy of McCarthy's *Blood Meridian* and read the passage about the Comanche attack.

I had never heard anything like it.

The writing was powerful—stripped down, epic, vivid, brutal, and beautiful all at the same time. I have been reading, rereading, studying, teaching, and enjoying McCarthy's works ever since.

Over the last fifteen years, McCarthy has become a more recognizable presence in American and world literature. His authorial voice stretches and pulls the genre of the American novel into new territory—sometimes with a single sentence. He published his first novel, *The Orchard Keeper*, in 1965. But until the early twenty-first century, he has been a relatively obscure American author. The slow rise of his reputation is due, in part, to his legendary reclusiveness. He has granted a handful of interviews over the course of his career to speak with members of the media. In 2007, two months after he won the Pulitzer Prize for his novel *The Road*, Oprah Winfrey aired an interview with him. That interview made McCarthy more accessible by providing the reading public with a biography to attach to his remarkable novels.

This book will discuss key details of his life in relation to his works. The first chapter, which is biographical, has been gleaned from interviews, reviews, articles, and conversations. By taking stock of those resources, I relate his remarkable rise to national prominence. His compelling life hovers over all of his novels, and while his biography does inform his work, I will show how those two elements diverge at various points. To become the major figure that he has, McCarthy has certainly done more than write about his own life—he has cultivated a powerful imagination and developed virtuosity in a variety of prose styles. Chapter 2 introduces these elements to new readers and contributes to the ongoing conversation about the author and his work.

McCarthy writes from the perspective of the self-exiled outcast. In this way, he has understood and created fiction on his own terms. Meaning is the province of authority, and McCarthy is not interested in making people obedient to intellect. In fact, the development of his own intellect was taken outside of all institutions except for, maybe, the Catholic Church. McCarthy's embrace, rejection, and renunciation of Catholicism is one of the more remarkable features of his later works and will be discussed in the chapters about specific works. In addition to analyzing such themes as his treatment of Catholicism, I will incorporate critical discussion of other major themes in the chapters that summarize his works.

The greater portion of this book (chapters 3–12) is a chronological analysis of McCarthy's primary genre, the novel. McCarthy is most famous for his ten novels: *The Orchard Keeper, Outer Dark, Child of God, Suttree, Blood Meridian, All the Pretty Horses, The Crossing, Cities of the Plain, No Country for Old Men,* and *The Road*. The text devotes a complete chapter to each of these major works wherein their themes, characters, and settings are explored. Each chapter will address how McCarthy's prose style has changed over time and how he has employed the conventions of the novel. There has been a lot of strong scholarship on his works, and I have appraised it and done my best to add to and not to replicate previous scholarship.

His plays, while not as popular as the novels, are significant in that they contain some of McCarthy's finest writing and most compelling subject matter. Chapter 13 discusses his three published plays: *The Gardener's Son* (which was a teleplay for PBS), *The Stonemason,* and *The*

Sunset Limited. These dramas prominently feature black Americans, and while they have a place in McCarthy's philosophical tradition, these works also add to McCarthy's pessimistic concerns about human nature.

Chapter 14 focuses on the intersection between McCarthy's works and contemporary issues. While McCarthy's novels portray an early twentieth-century America in which cowboys, rural settings, and romantic loners figure prominently, there also are substantial engagements with contemporary issues such as the war on drugs and nuclear war. This duality—that is, a willingness to be topical as well as exploring transcendent values such as heroism, truth, religion, and God—is one reason for the intense loyalty and interest of McCarthy's readership.

In chapter 15 on McCarthy and popular culture, I discuss movie adaptations and the relation of screenplays to his novels when relevant. Two of McCarthy's books, *All the Pretty Horses* and *No Country for Old Men,* have been made into movies. *The Road* is also in production at the writing of this book. Adaptations of his novels will present opportunities for McCarthy scholars. Because novels are notoriously difficult to adapt well into movies, scholars will study the interpretations of filmmakers in relation to the novels. McCarthy's most controversial and critically acclaimed book, *Blood Meridian,* also has had its movie rights purchased.

Chapter 16 on McCarthy's Internet presence is, by nature, contradictory as the author admits to writing on a typewriter. While aware of the Internet and his presence on it, he claims never to have looked at anything having to do with him or his works. Furthermore, when asked if he would approve or disapprove of the founding of the Cormac McCarthy Society, his only request was that he not be involved. This society meets annually, sells critical works, and has launched a Web site, http://www.cormacmccarthy.com, which is devoted to the promotion, scholarship, and appreciation of his works.

While Cormac McCarthy's legendary status as literary outsider prevents any sort of in-depth biography, his interviews have been incredibly significant. Interestingly enough, his interview with Oprah is probably the most revealing and comprehensive one that he has given. Other important interviews discussed in chapter 17 include ones done by *Vanity Fair* and the *New York Times Review of Books*. There have also been a number of reviews of McCarthy's work, but one of the most compelling, which I will discuss, is Michael Chabon's review of *The Road.*

While this book will be a guide to recognize and to appreciate the themes, literary traditions, and biographical connections in his novels, the best thing readers can do is read his work. When people tell me that they will read one of his books, they invariably say that I will have to explain it to them afterward. Certainly, there is meaning to be had in any of his novels, but the experience of reading them is also a form of meaning.

Chapter 18 concludes this text with a discussion of works that would be of interest to McCarthy's readers in terms of subject matter and style. McCarthy certainly has a fondness for American cinema, which is recognizable when looking at the development of his prose in the last three novels. Also, McCarthy's own work testifies to the fact that books are often responses to other books. He clearly was inspired by and admires Melville and Faulkner. In addition to the work of such established authors, I will discuss some contemporary writers who might be of interest to McCarthy enthusiasts.

It has been great fun to experience the phenomenal ascendance of McCarthy from little-known regional author to national figure. Because of my writing this book, my ninety-one-year-old grandmother (who was something of an equestrienne) read *All the Pretty Horses*. She has since read more of his novels. So, as scholarly and popular interest in the works of Cormac McCarthy continues to grow, I hope that this book will be an enduring guide to understanding and enjoying his body of work.

I

CORMAC McCARTHY: A WRITER'S LIFE

Cormac McCarthy is renowned for his reclusiveness and his disdain for literary circles. His refusals of lecture money and academic appointments have become legendary, mainly because they would have eased the grinding poverty that defined the first several decades of his adult life. McCarthy's self-imposed isolation forged his image as a rebellious writer who cared nothing for the trappings of literary success or notoriety. Because he deliberately rejected living the public life of a writer, his rise to national prominence is remarkable.

In 2007, McCarthy received his greatest literary achievement to date. His postapocalyptic novel, *The Road*, was awarded the Pulitzer Prize in fiction. Yet, scant biographical information exists about the author. For most of his writing career, he has actively shunned the public spotlight. McCarthy has granted only a handful of interviews to professional journalists in his lifetime. Two of those interviews were with the same person, arts critic Richard B. Woodward. Woodward interviewed McCarthy in 1992 for the *New York Times Book Review* as a preview for *All the Pretty Horses*, the first book for which McCarthy won widespread national acclaim. At the beginning of this piece, Woodward explains that McCarthy agreed to the interview only after securing a promise from his literary agent that he wouldn't have to do another one "for many years." Thirteen years and three novels later, Woodward sat down again with

McCarthy on the eve of the publication of his ninth novel, *No Country for Old Men*. In both interviews, Woodward comments about McCarthy's utter reluctance to share details from his personal life.

As a result of this aversion to media coverage, McCarthy's introduction to the general reading public comes belatedly in what is now an expansive writing career. McCarthy published his first novel in 1965. He published four subsequent novels in the years before *All the Pretty Horses*. None of those books sold more than five thousand copies in hardcover. His vocation has spanned more than four decades and produced ten novels, two stage plays, and one screenplay. Over the course of those years, he developed cult hero status among a small group of scholars and literary aficionados. Only in the early twenty-first century has he emerged in the broader public spectrum as the heir apparent of an American literary tradition that counts William Faulkner, Flannery O'Connor, Herman Melville, and others as its founders.

Three distinctive eras in McCarthy's life define his evolution as an American writer. The first era covers the period from 1933 (the year he was born) to 1965 (the year he published his first novel). The second covers the ten-year period (1965–1976) that he spent in and around Knoxville. The third section considers the period from 1976 (the year he left Knoxville) to the present.

1933–1965

McCarthy lived a life of relative poverty for most of his adult life. There is a certain irony to McCarthy's self-imposed poverty as he was the son of an affluent Washington lawyer who moved the McCarthy family to Tennessee from Rhode Island in 1937. At the time, Cormac (born Charles Jr.) was only four years old. McCarthy's father had taken a job as a lawyer for the Tennessee Valley Authority. This move would be a seminal event in shaping Cormac McCarthy's perspective as a writer. In Tennessee, he met and became friends with many of the people who would influence and even appear in his first four novels.

Living in rural Tennessee made a strong impression on McCarthy. Despite the Southern surroundings, the family kept its Irish-Gaelic sense of identity. His nickname, Cormac, is the Gaelic version of Charles and was reportedly bestowed on him by his father's aunts. Young Cormac was sent to Catholic school in Knoxville in the 1940s. He grew up, then, as a displaced Irish Catholic Northerner.

Because so little is known about Cormac McCarthy's early years, the few details that are available become more poignant. A 2005 article by

Richard B. Woodward about McCarthy published in *Vanity Fair* includes a few pictures of the author as a young child. The pictures capture a comfortable childhood that seems both idyllic and innocent. Images of McCarthy as a young boy in a canoe, in a family picture, and in a cowboy suit suggest a childhood filled with the ordinary trappings of postwar youth, but one that was also privileged.

In his 1992 interview with Woodward published in the *New York Times Book Review*, McCarthy spoke briefly about his pre–high school days and shared a story about how he struggled with show-and-tell. So many subjects interested him that he could not decide what to bring. Woodward describes how McCarthy claimed that he had so many hobbies, he could have given one to each of his classmates and still had many left over. From an early age, young Cormac found the world to be an endlessly fascinating place. This curiosity would manifest itself in his reading and in his writing.

He was the oldest of six children, and since his father had graduated at the top of his class in law school at Yale, in all likelihood, Gladys (his mother) and Charles Sr. had high expectations for young Charles. One of his brothers did go to law school and still practices in Knoxville. Life for the McCarthy family was comfortable, particularly compared with the abject poverty in which many of his neighbors lived. At a time when the country was recovering from the Great Depression, the McCarthy home had maids.

McCarthy befriended other students who attended the same Catholic school. An article, written by Mike Gibson and published in the Knoxville newspaper *Metro Pulse*, identifies many of his friends and recounts some of their escapades. With these friends, McCarthy roamed the surrounding environs of Knoxville, enjoying the wilderness of such places as Brown's Mountain and Red Mountain. Gibson's article also recounts an episode where McCarthy and his siblings dragged mattresses out of his family's house and spent the night out on the front lawn. As he grew older, his fondness for the outdoors grew into a deliberate commitment to the more austere aspects of living with nature.

McCarthy has said that if you grow up in the South you are going to see violence. Although he provided no examples of the brutality he witnessed, the savage elements in his novels suggest that he must have had some exposure to extreme poverty and violence while living in rural Tennessee. However, the known anecdotes about McCarthy's youth tend toward the precocious rather than the violent. For example, when he was a boy, he and a friend rolled huge boulders that weighed between five hundred and a thousand pounds down the side of a mountain.

He graduated from Knoxville's Catholic High in 1951. It was the last academic degree he earned, although not his last foray into formal education. He enrolled briefly at the University of Tennessee (1951–1952), dropped out, and spent four years in the Air Force (1953–1957). While enlisted, he was stationed in Alaska where he ran a radio show. During his years in the military, he began reading widely in fiction and philosophy, although he has never shared his reading list with the public.

Upon his discharge from the service in 1957, he returned to Knoxville and enrolled again at the University of Tennessee. He studied physics and engineering before leaving college a second time two years later. While in school, he learned much about editing and writing from an editing job he landed through the GI Bill. An English professor at the university, Robert Daniel, paid McCarthy to edit his book of eighteenth-century English essays. In doing the work for Daniel's textbook, McCarthy claims to have developed his distaste for the semicolon and his sparse employment of punctuation. His editing work pleased his professor, and McCarthy came to the realization that punctuation is not essential to clear writing. He has applied this philosophy to all of his novels. Consequently, McCarthy's lack of punctuation should be understood as a deliberate stylistic stance rather than a rebellious disdain for convention.

Although McCarthy did not stay long enough at university to earn a degree, he did publish two short stories in a student journal, "A Wake for Susan" and "A Drowning Incident." Other early successes included two awards for his writing, which he received from the Ingram-Merrill Foundation in 1959 and 1960. Perhaps these successes convinced McCarthy to abandon his course of study in physics and engineering and begin making his life as a writer. He withdrew from the university for the last time in 1959.

While at school, McCarthy met a fellow student, Lee Holleman. In 1961 they married. Soon thereafter, their son, Cullen, was born. That same year, McCarthy and Holleman moved to Chicago where he worked part time in a used auto parts warehouse. He also began writing *Suttree*, which eventually became his fourth published novel.

McCarthy's stint in Chicago ended soon after it began. So did his marriage to Holleman. They divorced, and the author became completely estranged from his former spouse and their son. With his first marriage over, McCarthy roamed the South, including parts of North Carolina and the city of New Orleans. Specific details from this post-Holleman era are murky. McCarthy told journalist Garry Wallace, in his essay "Meeting McCarthy," that he spent an entire year during this time playing pool with friends.

By the mid-1960s, he had returned to haunting the nether-regions of Knoxville, collecting the colorful experiences that he eventually recounted in *Suttree*. While he roamed, McCarthy must have been writing because in 1965, his first book, *The Orchard Keeper*, was published by Random House. The author was thirty-two.

1965–1976

McCarthy submitted *The Orchard Keeper* to Random House, because it was the only publishing house he knew of. He also knew that Albert Erskine, William Faulkner's long-time editor, worked there. McCarthy had no literary agent and had submitted the novel blindly—he was completely unknown and unread outside of Tennessee.

After the publication of *The Orchard Keeper*, McCarthy slowly started to garner a small scholarly and even smaller popular following, but he would not receive widespread acclaim until almost thirty years after this first book. What is amazing is that he not only persevered during these years, but also wrote some magnificent novels. In addition to shunning speaking and teaching engagements, he also did not grant interviews. In fact, he still does not like associating with contemporary writers, which is somewhat reminiscent of Robert Frost, who referred to contemporary poets as "contemptuary." Despite his aversion to the public side of writing, he has said to have learned a tremendous amount from reading the novels of certain writers, among them William Faulkner, Herman Melville, and Fyodor Dostoyevsky.

The publication of *The Orchard Keeper* earned McCarthy the Faulkner Foundation Award for a first novel. He then parlayed his success with the Faulkner Award into a traveling grant from the American Academy of Arts and Letters. With these funds, he made plans to tour Europe including a stop in his family's homeland, Ireland. There, he intended to see Blarney Castle, which was built in the fifteenth century by King Cormac, the first king of Ireland. McCarthy's trip may have been an homage to the muse of writerly inspiration. Blarney Castle is the site of the legendary Blarney Stone, said to impart the powers of eloquence and persuasion.

En route to Ireland on the cruise ship *Sylvania*, McCarthy met Anne DeLisle, a British former United Service Organizations (USO) performer. She and McCarthy fell in love and traveled together across Europe. They were married in England in 1966. They bought a Jaguar and drove it around France until it broke down in Paris, where McCarthy repaired it. The couple spent time in England, Ireland, Italy, Paris and southern France, and Barcelona and Ibiza in Spain, where McCarthy joined a writer's colony.

On Ibiza, he wrote *Outer Dark*, his second published novel. This book firmly established him as part of the Southern gothic literary tradition for its use of irony and the grotesque to explore cultural issues. The violence and rural poverty McCarthy creates in this book bear utterly no resemblance to the cosmopolitan lifestyle he and DeLisle were leading. McCarthy's money eventually ran out until he received a grant from the Rockefeller Foundation, which allowed him to spend two more years in London and Paris with DeLisle. In 1968, two years after he completed the novel, *Outer Dark* was published.

After this extended European stint, DeLisle and McCarthy returned to Knoxville in the late 1960s and began to live a Spartan life. McCarthy was drinking heavily during this time. Alcoholism and privation became more than themes that resonated in McCarthy's works from this era. They were the defining elements of his existence.

This spare life in Knoxville with DeLisle did have its comic moments. DeLisle was well liked by McCarthy's friends, in spite of the fact that one of them said that because of her British accent, she "don't speak 'Anglish' too good." While McCarthy wrote, she provided the bare necessities for the couple's survival by running a diner in Knoxville called Annie's.

In the *New York Times* interview with Richard B. Woodward, DeLisle recalled her time in Knoxville with her then husband. She said they lived for eight years in a dairy barn on the outskirts of the city. They had no running water and bathed in the lake. They ate lots of beans. DeLisle recounted how McCarthy would be invited to lecture about his book at university for a couple of thousand dollars. McCarthy would refuse. They would eat more beans.

Between 1965 and 1976, McCarthy completed two novels—*Outer Dark* and *Child of God*. He also continued to write and rewrite *Suttree,*

In his interviews, Cormac McCarthy invokes the poverty and hardship he suffered while developing his writing career. His talent seems to have ensured his survival, often at the final hour. He shared an anecdote with David Kushner in an interview published in *Rolling Stone* about a courier showing up at his door. McCarthy had just eaten the last store of food from his freezer, and he said he thought the guy was there to arrest him for something. Not so. The courier handed him a check for $20,000 from a private donor who admired his work.

which scholars generally agree to be his most autobiographical novel. The eponymous protagonist spends years toiling as a fisherman and engaging in bouts of heroic drinking before leaving Knoxville. DeLisle typed this eight-hundred-page manuscript not once but twice.

McCarthy eventually made upgrades to the dairy barn by building a fireplace using stones salvaged from fellow Knoxville native James Agee's house. Agee earned a posthumously awarded Pulitzer Prize in 1957 for his autobiography, *A Death in the Family*. At the time McCarthy was scavenging stones for a fireplace, Agee's house had been razed as part of an urban renewal project.

McCarthy's construction of the fireplace has thematic resonance beyond serving as a functional memorial to Agee and his work. In the *New York Times* interview with Woodward, McCarthy said that "stacking up stones is the oldest trade there is" and that with the advent of hydraulic cement this ancient trade is moving close to extinction. He claimed to have learned stonemasonry while working in the South with a family of black stonemasons. These experiences formed the basis for his 1994 play, *The Stonemason*.

Few photos of McCarthy from this decade in Knoxville exist in the public record. The first edition of *The Orchard Keeper* includes a portrait of a young-looking McCarthy that has not been reproduced elsewhere. The next photo from this era, which has entered the record, ran with Woodward's 2005 piece in *Vanity Fair*. The photo depicts a comfortable looking man in his home in Rockford, Tennessee. These two pictures belie his past, present, and future obscurity and poverty that followed him from Knoxville to El Paso.

Another photo of McCarthy is included in a collection of essays by Mark Morrow called *Images of the Southern Writer* published in 1985. Morrow tracked down the reclusive McCarthy with the help of his editor, Albert Erskine. Erskine wrote the introduction to Morrow's book, which is why, in all probability, he revealed the whereabouts of his notoriously elusive client. After months of looking for McCarthy, Morrow finally found him living in a ten-by-ten hotel room in Knoxville. McCarthy was, obviously, in the throes of writing. Morrow cryptically said that it was "obvious" that he could not take his picture in his hotel room. He photographed McCarthy in an old railroad station in Knoxville that was characterized by Knoxville's homeless and their refuse. Interestingly, the photo Morrow includes is undated. Morrow mentions a 1982 grant that McCarthy won, and, because the book was published in 1985, we can assume that the photograph was taken in the intervening years. It was during this time that McCarthy was writing his masterpiece, *Blood Meridian*.

McCarthy seems to have a penchant for small rentals like the one in which Morrow found him in Knoxville. McCarthy has said that he lived out of cheap hotel rooms in New Orleans, in North Carolina, and in other places around the South. In the *New York Times* interview, Woodward asked him whether he ever paid alimony to his first wife. McCarthy suggested he was too poor and recounted a story of being evicted from a $40-a-month room in New Orleans for nonpayment of rent.

Sometime around 1974 or shortly thereafter, McCarthy left Knoxville. He left without DeLisle. In 1976, McCarthy moved to El Paso, Texas, where he has said he quit drinking while living with a girlfriend in deliberate obscurity. DeLisle and McCarthy officially divorced in 1981. She moved to Florida, and in the early 1990s, she was running a restaurant.

1976 TO PRESENT

By the time McCarthy had relocated to Texas, his adult life had been one of toiling in poverty and relative obscurity, with the added complication of engaging in hard drinking. Of his drinking days in Knoxville, McCarthy has said that the people he knew either quit drinking or died. McCarthy had been writing for twenty years and had published only three novels: *The Orchard Keeper, Outer Dark,* and *Child of God.* He had been drinking continuously for around twenty-five years, his first two marriages had ended, and he had abandoned Tennessee for Texas.

McCarthy, the transplanted Northerner, moved from the South to the Southwest. The move is the culmination of a lifetime of interest in the mythology of the American West. In an article by David Kushner published in the December 27, 2007, issue of *Rolling Stone,* McCarthy cites the global popularity of the American West and its lore, arguing that they have even heard of cowboys in Mongolia. And Anne DeLisle has said that McCarthy always thought he would write a great Western.

As much as McCarthy is influenced by Faulkner, an equally important influence in his work is the idea of the West as it exists in American culture. Inside a small white adobe house behind a shopping mall in El Paso, McCarthy realized this vision. He finished five novels that introduced his distinctive perspective on the American West: *Suttree* (1979), *Blood Meridian* (1985), and the Border Trilogy (*All the Pretty Horses,* 1992; *The Crossing,* 1994; and *Cities of the Plain,* 1998). All five of these books evoke a world that is distinctively male, rife with gory violence, and stripped of almost any invocation of psychological motivators. Men kill each other to survive in this mythologized world.

During these years in El Paso, McCarthy regained much of the momentum that characterized his early writing career. The publication of *Suttree* in 1979 marked the completion of a novel that took him twenty years to write. After publication of this encyclopedic and virtuosic work, fellow author Saul Bellow recommended him for a MacArthur Fellowship (the so-called genius awards). This grant provided McCarthy the means to do the years of research that were required to write *Blood Meridian*, a book some consider to be his masterpiece and one of the great works in American literature. When it was published in 1985, it sold around 1,500 copies and quickly went out of print. At this time, McCarthy reportedly possessed only a car and a typewriter, which may or may not be the same typewriter he still uses. In 1992, he told Woodward that he "likes computers," but apparently he doesn't like them enough to use them for writing. His latest novel, *The Road,* he composed on a typewriter.

The few years following publication of *Blood Meridian* would be the last time in McCarthy's life that he would be famously unknown. The little that is known about the years before the publication of *All the Pretty Horses* replicates what we know about the past. McCarthy continued to turn down interviews, kept playing pool, ate in cafeterias and diners, and did his laundry in a Laundromat.

This time in El Paso also signals a tremendous shift in his prose and also the nature of his relationship to the public. Even though *Blood Meridian* had gone out of print, its reputation was steadily growing. In El Paso, as he fended off more requests for interviews, he acquired, for the first time in his life, a literary agent, Amanda Urban, who is still his agent and guards his privacy closely. She helped convince him to do a bit of publicity for his novels. She orchestrated the interview with Woodward and the *New York Times Book Review* in 1992 just before the release of *All the Pretty Horses*. As a result, the book was the first of McCarthy's to register widely with the public. This attention culminated with McCarthy winning the National Book Award and the National Book Critics Circle Award in 1992.

McCarthy followed the success of *All the Pretty Horses* with *The Crossing* in 1994. An excerpt of this novel appeared in an issue of *Vanity Fair*. In 1998, McCarthy published the final installment of The Border Trilogy, *Cities of the Plain*. The novel was not as well received as the previous two. McCarthy began the book as a screenplay, a format which helped to spawn the minimalist writing style that became a hallmark of McCarthy's more mature work.

If the first four decades of McCarthy's life are marked by a deliberate evasion of the public spotlight, in the start of his fifth decade, his stance toward publicity has softened substantially. The year 2005 ushered in

McCarthy's status as a national icon. In 2005, before the publication of *No Country for Old Men*, he sat down again for an interview with Woodward. The interview was published in *Vanity Fair*. McCarthy's book, a noir Western, was adapted for film by the popular filmmaking team Joel and Ethan Coen. Among a prolific repertoire of offbeat films, including *Raising Arizona, Barton Fink, Fargo*, and *The Big Lebowski*, *No Country for Old Men* proved to be the Coen brothers' biggest hit with the academy to date, garnering eight Oscar nominations and winning four. With the success of the film, McCarthy's appeal reached an even more expansive audience.

With his reputation as an American writer at its apex, in March 2007 McCarthy received the Pulitzer Prize for his tenth published novel, *The Road*. Shortly thereafter, McCarthy participated in an hour-long television interview with media mogul Oprah Winfrey. The interview was conducted at the Santa Fe Institute (SFI), a cutting-edge scientific think tank founded by Nobel Prize winning physicist Murray Gell-Mann. McCarthy is a permanent fellow at SFI and the institute's only writer. In David Kushner's article for *Rolling Stone,* McCarthy reveals that he has been visiting the SFI since 1992.

His position at SFI is a natural fit for a polymath like McCarthy. Kushner's article indicates that McCarthy is highly esteemed by his colleagues. In fact, he is the only person at the institute without a doctorate. One resident has said that it is easier to talk to McCarthy about the work that other scientists are doing rather than talking to the scientists. *The Road* and *No Country for Old Men* both were composed while McCarthy was a fellow at the SFI. *The Road* draws on conversations that McCarthy had with paleobiologist Doug Erwin on the subject of extinction and the potential results of a nuclear holocaust.

Despite McCarthy having been such an obscure personality for so much of his life, McCarthy's readers now are able to connect some of his interests with his works. His interviews since the publication of *No Country for Old Men*, in fact, often reveal more about the goings-on at SFI than they reveal about the author's novels. Though he maintains his privacy and a respectful distance from the media, McCarthy has a

McCarthy is the quintessentially displaced American author. Novelist Clyde Edgerton recounted an anecdote shared by a friend of his who once spoke with McCarthy. Edgerton's friend said McCarthy claimed that he never really liked anywhere he'd lived.

reputation for gregariousness within his chosen circle of friends, family, and colleagues. Rather than seeing his rejection of most kinds of critical attention in a pessimistic light, he has said that his obscurity has been a necessary protection of his creative powers. McCarthy has indicated a belief in the power of the unconscious, especially as it pertains to writing. Constant public interruptions, by implication, would prevent the subconscious from working on the ideas of the conscious mind.

The dynamic between private and public is changing with McCarthy's third marriage to a woman named Jennifer Winkley. He and Winkley have a son, John Francis McCarthy, who was named for McCarthy's grandfather. McCarthy's novel *The Road* is dedicated to his son. McCarthy, Winkley, and son John live in Santa Fe, New Mexico. In January 2008, Texas State University at San Marcos acquired all of McCarthy's papers, which include notes, drafts, and personal correspondence.

McCarthy, now in his seventh decade, seems to be as settled as he has ever been. He admits that he has spent most of his life avoiding work, which he has said, with some humor and irony, was difficult. He signed a two-book deal with Knopf, so he must have some finished or partially finished manuscripts. He and Winkley own a home near Santa Fe, a town he refers to as a "theme park." His wife's sculpture adorns their front lawn, and his son's room is decorated with models and maps.

Having published ten novels, and having reached the age of 76, McCarthy's rise to fame seems more comprehensible. By remaining true to his own artistic and personal sensibilities, he has managed to produce novels of strong literary merit that are now finding a broad audience.

McCarthy has said that a writer should express "the soul of culture." As evidenced by how he has captured the popular and academic imagination, McCarthy has done just that. His independence, his rejection of a conventional life, his willingness to suffer, and his desire to achieve success on his own terms are quintessential aspects of American cultural identity in their romantic stoicism. This personal idealism runs counter to the pessimism embodied in his novels and in the author's own public comments. Through his work, McCarthy has explored the violation of basic taboos in our culture, such as incest, necrophilia, cannibalism, and infanticide. He claims to have written *The Road*, an allegory of survival in a postapocalyptic America, largely because of his belief that humans will cause their own extinction—and sooner rather than later.

Charged by some critics as being a "conservative," McCarthy is more aptly described as a classicist in that he examines the importance of cultural continuity and cultural destruction. McCarthy sees human nature as "fixed" and unable to be perfected by society. In McCarthy's fictive world, society is malleable, not human nature. When he correctly observes that beheadings have never been televised in our society, McCarthy's point is that human beings have been continuously committing grotesque acts of violence against each other since the beginning of time, but in contemporary Western society, that violence is no longer visible to the public. This conflict between the changeability of society and the fixed nature of human consciousness drives the narrative forces in much of his work. This fundamental aesthetic conflict will be explored in greater detail in a subsequent chapter.

DISCUSSION QUESTIONS

- Does McCarthy's rejection of personal contact disqualify him from being a public intellectual?
- How did McCarthy become famous by not being famous?
- How did alcoholism affect his writing?
- How did poverty influence his life?
- Why did McCarthy not want the trappings of fame?
- How does his version of the literary South differ from the literary Southwest?
- Why does McCarthy's interest in science have little or no influence on his work?
- McCarthy has lived most of his life without having a job. How difficult would it be to live without having a job?
- What does his writing say about the "soul of our culture?"
- How does being brought up Catholic influence his novels?

2

CORMAC McCARTHY AND THE GENRE

McCarthy, speaking with journalist Richard B. Woodward in 1992, said he believed that the novel can "encompass all the various disciplines and interests of humanity." That is a totemic endorsement from the legendary autodidact who said in the same interview, "Everything's interesting."

It is no wonder, then, that fiction is McCarthy's genre.

Fiction is one of three overarching categories used to classify literature; the other two are poetry and drama. And while McCarthy is like many contemporary writers in that he has produced works in other genres (he has published two stage plays and one screenplay), the novel is his most common and critically acclaimed format.

All of McCarthy's published novels—ten to date—rely on conventional features of fiction, specifically theme, character, structure, style, subgenre, and tradition. His approach to these six elements of fiction, in particular character and style, is highly innovative and has given rise to a distinctively "McCarthyian" technique.

To understand how McCarthy employs these elements of fiction requires a careful analysis of one of the six features: tradition. Literary tradition can be understood as the way in which authors adhere to the form and content of their predecessors. The literary traditions in which McCarthy writes provide a framework for understanding how the other five features function in his works.

The concept of literary tradition covers a broad range of literary works. Tradition can refer to something as general as the prose style of an author. It also can be as narrow as a kind of writing that is defined by time and place, such as the Victorian novel.

In McCarthy's own words, "Books beget books."

McCarthy's ten published books fall within three separate literary traditions: Southern gothic, the Western, and postapocalyptic. His first four novels, *The Orchard Keeper, Outer Dark, Child of God,* and *Suttree,* are Southern gothic. His next five, The Border Trilogy (*All the Pretty Horses, The Crossing,* and *Cities of the Plain*), *Blood Meridian,* and *No Country for Old Men,* are Westerns. His latest novel, *The Road,* for which he won the Pulitzer Prize in fiction in 2007, is postapocalyptic.

Though these published works suggest a chronological progression from one tradition to the next, there is no reason to believe that this progression was intentional or deliberate. The order in which his books were published might not reflect the order in which they were written. But then again, it might. McCarthy is deliberately elusive about his writing process.

While his books are part of clearly identifiable literary traditions, McCarthy's fiction has redefined the boundaries of all three. He has pushed these boundaries by challenging four of the genre's essential elements—theme, structure, character, and style—within each particular tradition. The result is an innovative body of work that is both within and beyond the conventions of the genre.

McCarthy's approach to the fictive element subgenre, however, is a different story. When referring to an element of fiction, subgenre is equivalent to subcategory. For example, if fiction is the genre, then subgenres of fiction would be romance, satire, horror stories, or science fiction. Subgenre typically refers to a broader categorization than does tradition, but there can be some overlap.

Literary criticism uses a number of terms to define the elements of fiction interchangeably. This approach has produced some disagreement about nomenclature in critical circles. Not everyone uses the term "subgenre" in the same way, for example. Couple this with the fact that all of the elements of fiction are interrelated and affect the development of one another, thereby further blurring the lines between them, and the language used to define these elements can seem even more obscure. Readers should be aware that these disagreements exist, but as long as the applied use of the terminology in context is clearly defined, these arguments should not be a barrier to understanding traditional and innovative elements in McCarthy's novels.

McCarthy's treatment of subgenre is marked by uniformity and sameness. All ten of McCarthy's published novels contain narrative elements of the *bildungsroman,* a German word that means "novel of growth or development." This is a classic kind of novel in which a youth, typically a young man, searches for a world view or unifying philosophy of life.

McCarthy's books evince a tragic narrative arc that proceeds as follows: a main character, always male, intentionally engages in action—often in the form of a quest—and is gradually destroyed by the convergence of events of his own making and of those beyond his control. The action that surrounds this main character is unusual for its violence, its exploration of social taboos, and its cast of secondary characters who typically lack human emotion. McCarthy's version of the *bildungsroman* immerses his readers in a fictive world dominated by men who are memorable mainly for the ultraviolent acts they commit against one another.

His treatment of character is one of the primary modes through which McCarthy expresses this distinctive vision of the American cultural experience. Characters in his books tend to exist as more than fictive personalities created for the purpose of entertaining the reader by propelling a narrative. McCarthy's characters are often symbolic creations; they function as direct links to themes being explored in the novel. These symbolic characters reflect how McCarthy has abandoned the contemporary use of social realism as a narrative approach in favor of stylistic structures that embrace forms that are more common to classical Greek tragedies and epics and the Bible.

Character development sparks one of the most striking differences between fiction and other genres. The main difference between fiction and drama or poetry is that all fiction is mediated. Unlike characters in a play or the speaker in a poem, characters in a fiction story cannot speak to the reader and their thoughts cannot be communicated without some type of mediation. This mediation is defined in terms of point of view, which is either subjective or objective. Through the subjective view, the fictive world is portrayed as it is experienced through the perspective of a singular protagonist. Through the objective view, which is also called the omniscient perspective, the author presents a narrative from multiple points of view in a neutral manner. McCarthy employs both of these techniques in his distinctive approach to expressing universal themes that affect the collective American soul.

As mentioned, social realism is a narrative mode that has been prevalent in fiction for the last two hundred years. This technique includes accurate, realistic representations of events from ordinary life. Novels in the social realist mode tend to rely on dialogue between characters to communicate the events that drive the arc of the story. Not so in McCarthy's works. He tends to employ an omniscient narrative perspective that favors mythic plots and features classical ideals. Characters in

McCarthy's stories confront timeless issues that have challenged human beings since the beginning of recorded history, such as the nature of evil in the world.

The discussion that follows builds on the general framework outlined above for understanding McCarthy's work by exploring in-depth McCarthy's use of subgenre and the other elements of fiction within the context of the Southern gothic, Western, and postapocalyptic literary traditions.

McCarthy and the Southern Gothic

McCarthy's Southern gothic novels are *The Orchard Keeper, Outer Dark, Child of God,* and *Suttree.* The Southern gothic literary tradition evolved from the antebellum South as an identifiable subgenre in American literature. It is a tradition embodied by writers including Flannery O'Connor, Tennessee Williams, and William Faulkner, the American author to whom McCarthy is most frequently compared. (McCarthy has been described as "the heir to Faulkner's throne.")

This intriguing subgenre features certain literary themes. One of these themes is a pervasive atmosphere of decay and despair. This sentiment relates directly to the South's defeat by the Union Army during the Civil War. The war radically altered the South's racist, slave-based economy. At war's end, the vicious legacy of racism stripped away the veneer of beauty and elegance and civilization, revealing what churned beneath Southern society: ugliness, debauchery, and the encroaching wilderness.

The atmosphere of decay in the Southern gothic tradition has a variety of manifestations in McCarthy's first four novels. Broadly speaking, McCarthy focuses on social transgressions—such as bootlegging, necrophilia, murder, rape, incest, cannibalism, infanticide, prostitution, and alcoholism—to create a vision of society that is falling apart. Some of these transgressions, such as bootlegging and alcoholism, can be seen as contemporary problems, but the other taboos reflect McCarthy's interest in the elemental and eternal problem of human depravity.

To explore this theme of decay within the Southern gothic tradition, McCarthy employs symbolic characters who desire a pastoral existence, engage in extreme violence, and are subjected to tragic narratives (in which McCarthy portrays the rise and fall of noble and ignoble characters). Through this thematic and stylistic combination, he sets himself apart from the dominant style of the twentieth-century novel, social realism.

Although characters in social realism often provide a vicarious experience for the reader, this is not true in McCarthy's work. Social realism tends to feature characters with whom the reader identifies so strongly that the reader experiences the story as that character. McCarthy's characters do not provide this kind of experience. His characters hearken back to the Bible or Homer's epics as figures who are trying to convey something about the mysterious process of suffering the elemental realities of life. He achieves this by rendering the psychology of the characters totally opaque and by imbuing them with traits that are unattractive, even repulsive. This denial of the vicarious experience for the reader separates McCarthy from most contemporary novelists.

In addition to creating characters with whom readers do not want to identify, McCarthy operates against other long-standing literary methods in his Southern gothic works. One of those methods is the use of the theme of the pastoral. The pastoral is an ancient thematic ideal that shows up in biblical lore as well as in literature from Greek and Roman culture. It is a theme that has remained essentially unchanged over time. The pastoral existence defines a mode of living in which the individual lives in harmony with nature in a rural setting completely apart from the corrupting elements of society. One of its main tenets is that it is an attainable and worthy goal.

Various characters in McCarthy's Southern gothic novels express a conscious or unconscious desire for this pastoral kind of life. But McCarthy undermines his characters by creating a fictive world in which the pastoral has never existed and will never exist. For McCarthy, the idea of Pastoral life is totally incompatible with Southern society. Harmony with nature is unattainable because all of Southern civilization, city and country, has been poisoned by endemic racism. Thus, McCarthy's characters are all confined to an inevitable, tragic arc.

This poison is embodied in McCarthy's work by the theme of violence. Violent elements continually destroy the possibility for any character to attain a pastoral existence. McCarthy pushes the degree of violence beyond normal heroics, in which there is a clear-cut winner and loser who determines the moral content of society. McCarthy's South is steeped in ultraviolence; his characters go far beyond the use of typical levels of force as a means to achieve what passes for justice in a ruined society. Necrophilia, rape, violent murder, and other carnage-laden violations occur because society is weak. Thus, McCarthy sees the destruction of the South as having altered society at its most basic level so that humans are free to indulge their most base instincts and compulsions. His fiction speaks of unredeemable moral decay on the social and individual level.

In addition to thematic conventions, the dissolution of society in Southern gothic novels is embodied by a cast of violent and disturbed characters who struggle to find their place throughout the narrative. The futility of this struggle is personified by the trope of the imbecile, which is another common feature of the Southern gothic tradition. The imbecile is a character born in a corrupted state, who often engages in corrupting behavior, and who is doomed to an inescapable fate, despite yearning for freedom from the corrupting elements of society.

McCarthy uses the figure of the imbecile to emphasize the debased atmosphere of the Appalachian South. The difference between McCarthy and other authors who have written in the Southern gothic tradition is that McCarthy's imbeciles are more vulgar, more violent, and more unredeemable than those who populate other books in the tradition.

Harper Lee, in her Southern gothic novel *To Kill a Mockingbird,* provides a memorable example of this type of character in Boo Radley. Radley is a simpleton. He is a weird recluse who arouses both fear and a spooky curiosity in neighborhood children. Despite all of the intrigue and suggestions of untoward behavior, Radley ultimately ends up being a force for good and moral righteousness in Lee's novel.

McCarthy's imbeciles are always bad. They embody different degrees of moral decay. In *Child of God,* the story's protagonist, Lester Ballard, is an imbecile-savant—he is the best shot in the county. However, Ballard is a serial killer and a necrophiliac. Ballard is not the most debased imbecilic character in the book. Ballard encounters an imbecile who is utterly without an identity. He is kept underneath a house and dies when Ballard sets fire to the house after killing the imbecile's mother. Ballard, the serial killer, in a perverse way, becomes the arbiter of moral justice when he kills this nameless idiot. McCarthy's Southern gothic novels are decadent, meaning they represent moral decay on the social and individual level.

In terms of style, decadence also refers to art that displays and emphasizes a highly ornate surface. McCarthy's combination of formal prose with debased subject matter confirms his status as a decadent novelist. In this decadent "art for art's sake" mode, McCarthy is not heavily invested in advocating for social causes in his novels. Nowhere is this more evident than with the theme of race.

McCarthy's work stands in sharp relief to the stand against white racism that is often portrayed by Southern gothic authors. McCarthy largely abandons black-white race relations as a theme in his fiction. In fact, racism only exists on the periphery of his Southern gothic novels. Racism in novelistic terms is the province of the aristocracy. Faulkner in his works dwells on the travails of that fallen class. In contrast, McCarthy's novels dwell exclusively on the underclass and its unemployed subcultures that carry the dim torch for the South's desire to be an innocent agrarian society. Many of McCarthy's characters are racist; they articulate the racism inherent in Southern culture. But none of his novels use black-white conflict to drive their narratives.

Instead of explicitly exploring racism as a main theme, McCarthy subjects his characters to the theme of nostalgia or "lost time." This convention takes many forms but is most notable as a simultaneous lament for and critique of the Old South and its doomed aristocratic class. In McCarthy, this convention appears as yearning for a simpler existence, particularly in relation to nature. As mentioned above, McCarthy alters this convention by eliminating the possibility that the South ever was or ever will be a pastoral refuge. Yet the concept of such a refuge persists as a powerful abstraction for all of his protagonists in all of his Southern novels. Again, the characters are doomed. Racism is the implicit cause of the tragedy, although this truth is not explicitly divulged.

A final convention of the Southern gothic tradition that deserves mention is the treatment of romantic love. In Southern gothic novels, romantic love is a common element; lover and beloved are joined in union. The union is typically ill-fated. McCarthy's works are wholly devoid of romantic love. Male-female relationships in his Southern gothic works are debased. They appear as a living arrangement with a prostitute in *Suttree*, as incest in *Outer Dark*, and as necrophilia in *Child of God,* and they are totally absent in the *Orchard Keeper*. The absence of romantic love in his quartet of Southern fiction demonstrates a departure from the tradition.

McCarthy's characters tend to inhabit predominantly masculine settings. His female characters are all flat. This absence of romantic love, then, relates to his deliberate or unconscious decision (it is unclear which) not to create female characters that are wholly realized. The absence of women in his stories limits McCarthy from joining the company of canonical writers such as Shakespeare and Faulkner. McCarthy's male characters, while they are complex, are not offset by any fully imagined female ones, and in this way, he not only departs from an important convention of modern fiction, but also limits the imaginative scope of his narratives.

In addition to altering the conventions of theme and character, McCarthy's Southern gothic novels break new stylistic ground. The prose style of his early work connects McCarthy to Faulkner, yet McCarthy eschews one of Faulkner's dominant modes of character development—that is, stream of consciousness. Faulkner frequently uses that literary device, which functions as an unstructured combination of memories, dreams, internal monologues, and associations, to develop an understanding of the interior life of a character, thereby expanding the narrative. In Faulkner's work, this technique often would obscure key details of the narrative, such as who is speaking to whom. Such narrative ambiguity is an example of modernist aesthetics.

McCarthy employs this type of narrative ambiguity in only one book, his first published novel, *The Orchard Keeper*. McCarthy uses stream of consciousness to intertwine the narratives of Marion Sylder and John Wesley Rattner. He uses this device to obscure the connection between the two—Marion has killed John's father, but neither of them ever discover this. Furthermore, the reader has to read the stream of consciousness passages closely to discover this important aspect of the story. The prose earned him strong reviews from Malcolm Cowley, Ralph Ellison, James Michener, and Robert Penn Warren. This combination of a Faulknerian style with pastoral subject matter showcased the talent of a young writer who was working with stylistic and thematic conventions that, although experimental at the time, were accepted by contemporary writers and critics.

McCarthy's nod to traditional stylistic techniques and his penchant for innovation is evident in the dialogue of his characters. He uses a blend of highly formal prose, colloquialisms, and authentic rural Southern dialect. At times, his characters speak in short, terse sentences that consist of only a few words—a minimalist prose that is reminiscent of Hemingway. Hemingway favored omission and ambiguity to imply significant meaning in unsaid content. For McCarthy, however, ambiguity in dialogue is not the objective. McCarthy's minimalist approach is designed to ensure that the dialogue conveys exactly what it contains.

In direct opposition to McCarthy's minimalist dialogue are the philosophical monologues that echo Shakespeare and the Baroque and that ornament his novels at one point or another. McCarthy's love of arcane knowledge and obscure words shows an awareness of a high culture that most of his characters never know anything about. While this particular irony may be lost on the reader, the juxtaposition does no damage to the novels. In fact, that dual aesthetic of high and low culture is a crucial stylistic innovation that is present in virtually all of his novels. The reader sees this high-low split when Suttree wanders into the wilderness of a nearby mountain. He crosses paths with a mountain resident, who is hunting. Suttree, in a hallucinatory delirium, is called "loony" by the man. Suttree, displaying class and philosophical superiority, says, "at least I exist."

Realistic and highly stylized dialogue is one way in which the reader experiences McCarthy's characters. McCarthy creates characters in such a manner so that they gain knowledge about the world, yet they are inherently static in that their experiences do not change their flaws. Rather, and this is true of all of his male characters, their flaws become intertwined with their virtues until the two are almost indistinguishable. Therefore, we see innocent characters destroyed or altered by evil characters, and those characters who are evil are inconsistently brought to justice. McCarthy's fixed characters reveal a certain set of opinions on the nature of humanity. That pessimistic view is at odds with the fact that cultures do change for the better at times.

At the end of the novel *Suttree*, the main character leaves Knoxville, Tennessee. In direct parallel, with the publication of his next novel, *Blood Meridian*, McCarthy leaves the Southern gothic tradition for the American Western. The protagonist of *Blood Meridian* is born in Tennessee and leaves for Texas, thereby completing the shift in tradition.

McCarthy and the Western

Despite the change in location symbolized by the birth of his nameless protagonist in *Blood Meridian* (he's known as "the kid"), McCarthy brings structural and thematic elements that he developed in the Southern gothic to the tradition of the American Western. Violence becomes even more amplified, the characters still seek a pastoral existence (particularly in The Border Trilogy), and the narrative arc is still unalterably tragic.

What further differentiates most of the Westerns from the Southern gothic is that romantic love becomes linked to the pastoral. This is an important innovation and is one way in which McCarthy adheres to the genre of the American Western. In other ways, he deviates radically from the conventions of the tradition.

McCarthy's later books, beginning with the publication of *Blood Meridian* in 1985 and including *All the Pretty Horses, The Crossing, Cities of the Plain,* and *No Country for Old Men*, can be loosely classified as part of the Western literary tradition. At the same time, they cannot.

In literary circles, the Western has been relegated to a lower caste of books known as "fiction as commercial product." Comparable traditions include spy novels, romances, and science fiction and share a common plot development and conflict resolution that relies on a formulaic structure. With his Western novels, Cormac McCarthy has contributed to the creation of a new class of Western fiction that is a literary tradition in its own right. McCarthy does not have a deep peer group of writers in this higher Western style. However, some contemporary authors who have helped elevate the Western to a higher literary form include fiction writers Annie Proulx and Wallace Stegner, and the nonfiction writing of Edward Abbey. (Abbey was a student of Stegner and, in his later years, an acquaintance of McCarthy.)

McCarthy's foray into the tradition of the Western is a significant development in the tradition's history. Before McCarthy's work, Westerns were the dual province of Hollywood (think *Bonanza*) and of popular fiction like the novels of Louis L'Amour, Zane Grey, and Larry McMurtry. McCarthy embraces conventional elements of the tradition, but he inverts the value system that created the tradition: Manifest Destiny. All of McCarthy's Westerns function to destroy America's illusion that Manifest Destiny was either benign or benevolent.

McCarthy's Westerns employ elements of the tradition: cowboys, an American West heavily influenced by Hispanic culture, ranches, Indians, the frontier, settlers, cavalry, the gunfighter, and what happens when all of these things collide. For McCarthy the collision unveils a loss of innocence for the young and old male protagonists. The *bildungsroman* subgenre drives the structure of the novels. Yet, he works against this convention by ensuring that, ultimately, all of his main characters fail or only partially succeed in their ambitions.

McCarthy's fascination with young male protagonists, while obvious in the Southern novels, becomes even more pronounced in the cowboy figures in his Westerns. McCarthy employs the cowboy archetype, the independent American male whose actions, lawful or not, are always justifiable. The cowboy is a familiar archetype to Americans. But McCarthy toys with our understanding of this quintessential character. Furthermore, McCarthy alters the cowboy's character by making cowboys anachronistic within the narratives he creates for them. For example his two protagonists, Billy Parham and John Grady Cole, are cowboys during the 1930s and 1940s, long after the frontier of the West had closed.

The tragic narrative arc on which McCarthy's cowboys are stuck resembles the arc in one of McCarthy's favorite novels, *Moby Dick*, which presents a distinctly womanless world that is quintessentially American. Following Leslie Fielder's analysis of American literature in his classic study, *Love and Death in the American Novel*, it is possible to see McCarthy along a continuum that includes Melville, Twain, Cooper, and Hawthorne—to name just a few novelists who portray young male protagonists who avoid permanent relationships with women. This may seem a bit simplistic, but a cursory look at McCarthy's novels shows young males continually in flight from male-female relationships. If young males do end up in relationships with women, McCarthy destroys the relationship and kills the male. This separation of the genders also shows him to be completely removed from the novel's mode of social realism, which shows men and women in contact with each other.

McCarthy's male protagonists are solitary characters. As such, they fit nicely into the "frontier" ideology of the American West in which the isolated individual is free to pursue his full identity. Yet, McCarthy works against the themes and ideals of the frontier that are commonly associated with the American West, such as independence, self-reliance, and most important, innocence. McCarthy's young cowboys are never victorious. They die young or die old and alone with attainment of the pastoral ideal held out of reach. Sometimes, it is just a little out of reach; sometimes it is so far away that it was never a realistic possibility. In these failed lives, McCarthy undermines the long-standing tradition of the triumphant male in the Western genre.

McCarthy's Westerns are replete with male characters; women, like in the Southern gothic novels, are almost nonexistent. When they do exist, their characters are flat. Despite this imbalance of gender in his novels, McCarthy's Westerns provide a substantial aesthetic experience. Instead of relying on character development and vicarious identification with the characters to engage his readers, McCarthy relies on the force of his narratives. His characters become symbolic. This crucial distinction between character as vicarious agent and character as symbolic presence in the narrative imbues McCarthy's characters with a stoic nobility that transcends the nature of the struggle.

The almost exclusively masculine world that the characters inhabit does not necessarily mean that the characters are happy. In fact, a devastating cosmic irony to the absence of female characters suggests that the crushing isolation many of his characters feel is due to their inability to understand or even want to understand women.

The brutal and unrelenting ways in which McCarthy destroys his secondary characters, isolates his protagonists, and denies all of them the fulfillment of their pastoral yearnings serve as McCarthy's indictment of Manifest Destiny. American identity is deeply rooted in a vision of the West as a place of opportunity and limitless potential. McCarthy's novels negate those historical traditions.

The way McCarthy addresses the defining aspects of Manifest Destiny in his Westerns—namely, the treatment of American Indians and Mexicans by whites—is similar to the way in which he treats black-white relations in his Southern gothic novels. Native Americans have varying degrees of importance and prominence in these novels. Quite frequently, they are cast as being just as violent as, if not more violent than, their Anglo rivals, with whom they struggle for supremacy on the contested lands of Texas, New Mexico, and Arizona. Native Americans in McCarthy's novels are rarely individualized; in fact, they are almost always presented in groups. As a result, the stories do not function as a commentary on race relations between people. Like his earlier works, his Western novels are a bloodletting, a catharsis. He says nothing overt about the nature of the Native American experience. He lets readers draw their own conclusions.

The story that drives *Blood Meridian* is one of merciless genocidal westward expansion. The consequences of this bloody process are what doom the ranch, the quintessential pastoral ideal of the American West, to a failed state in McCarthy's subsequent novels. McCarthy's Westerns are peppered by the ruined and abandoned dreams of ranchers. The pastoral is gone, unattainable. As in his Southern gothic works, Western society is debased and irredeemable. Like the Southern plantation, the glory of Western expansion is, at its core, dishonorable.

McCARTHY AND POSTAPOCALYPTIC LITERATURE

After exploring the Western tradition, McCarthy moves into new territory with *The Road*. The narrative is sparse, unburdened by the cultural and historical details that were present in the Southern gothic and Western novels. He adheres more closely to two of the elements of fiction, character and narrative style. And McCarthy extends his thematic reach to broach a universal theme that appears in all of his work—the nature of evil in the world—within a distinctly contemporary context.

In *The Road*, a catastrophic event destroys civilization. The novel follows a father and his seven-year-old son as they make their way, alone, through a horrifically wasted landscape in hopes of reaching coastal waters to survive the increasingly harsh winters.

The subgenre of apocalyptic literature has a long tradition that includes many popular and serious works, which can be seen from the beginning of literary history in the Book of Revelation to Stephen King's epic apocalyptic novel, *The Stand*. *The Road*, however, takes the subgenre of apocalyptic literature and strips away its strongest and most basic convention: a final battle between good and evil that will decide the fate of humanity once and for all. McCarthy's stark and arresting story depicts humans persevering in a decimated world, after the battle has been lost. Consequently, the characters' struggle is futile: the only hope that exists is surviving for another day. By taking away that convention of final cosmic reckoning, where good finally defeats evil for eternity, McCarthy has created a starkly powerful story about the consequences of environmental and social collapse.

McCarthy's narrative style in *The Road* may be the most fully realized of his novels in that it is distinctly his own. His other novels echo the style of his predecessors—Faulkner, Hemingway, Melville—but in this novel, McCarthy's technique is so innovative that he has flushed out the ghosts of other authors. The narrative is simple and is rendered in McCarthy's most sparse prose to date. This minimalist approach has a beguiling effect: it communicates tremendously powerful and complex emotions with few words.

Interestingly, in this novel in which hope is not part of the narrative equation and the stylistic technique is uncomplicated, McCarthy renders his most psychologically alive protagonist. In *The Road*, McCarthy dabbles in social realism by rendering an emotional interior for the character of the unnamed father. The father loves his son. That is without doubt. For the first time, in this bare-bones novel about living through hell on earth, McCarthy reveals the heart of his protagonist.

DISCUSSION QUESTIONS

- What is the difference between a structural and a thematic convention?
- What is the pastoral?
- Why is narrative so important to McCarthy's novels?
- Why does McCarthy obscure the psychology of his characters?
- Why do McCarthy's novels avoid the "happy" ending?
- What typical conventions of the Western does McCarthy use and not use?
- How does McCarthy treat violence?
- What is social realism in fiction?
- How does McCarthy use the Bible in his novels?

3

THE ORCHARD KEEPER
(1965)

Cormac McCarthy's first book, *The Orchard Keeper*, was published in 1965 when the author was thirty-two years old. In this first novel, McCarthy deploys the major themes and stylistic techniques that will persist as hallmarks in his future works. Page numbers cited from *The Orchard Keeper* are from the 1993 paperback edition (New York: First Vintage International).

In *The Orchard Keeper*, McCarthy unfurls two primary themes: the first is a constant yearning for a pastoral existence; the second is a view of the natural world order that is dominated by violence, corruption, privation, and, ultimately, decline. This latter theme ensures a tragic narrative arc for McCarthy's protagonists, all of whom are men. Evil and corruption abound and render the pastoral forever unattainable.

This book also introduces the first iteration of McCarthy's distinctive approach to narrative. The story in *The Orchard Keeper* is told by an omniscient third-person narrator. This unknown and unknowable narrative entity becomes the lynchpin of McCarthy's distinctive stylistic techniques.

The narrator provides colorful, full-page, single paragraph descriptions of time, place, and action. Like the narrative voice used by William Faulkner, the narrator in *The Orchard Keeper* demonstrates a command of language and vocabulary that is distinctly unlike the speech of the

> First Editions of *The Orchard Keeper* are rare and can command between $1,000 and $5,000 on the rare book market. I own a first edition of this novel, which a friend of mine gave to me when I was in graduate school. This friend purchased the novel for a dollar at a library book sale in 1997. It still had the library card jacket in it. The book had never been checked out since the library acquired it. The dust jacket of the book includes a rare picture of the author that has just been put on the Cormac McCarthy Society Web site. The dust jacket also has the original blurbs by Ralph Ellison, Malcolm Cowley, James A. Michener, and Robert Penn Warren.

characters, which is recounted in heavy dialect and recreates the parlance and cadence of Appalachia. But McCarthy pushes Faulkner's style one step further: McCarthy never uses quotation marks to differentiate his characters' speech from the narrative passages. Without quotation marks, characters' thoughts and speech merge into the narrative voice. The result is that the story evokes the ancient form of the epic, like the stories in the Bible or in Homer's *Odyssey*, where the narrative employs an elevated language to tell the story of a particular character.

That story in *The Orchard Keeper* is the coming-of-age story of a young man named John Wesley Rattner. Like all of McCarthy's novels, Rattner's story follows a tragic narrative arc. He and the other characters are condemned to a corrupt, excessively violent, unsavory world that is in a state of active decline.

The story is set in and around Knoxville, Tennessee, during the mid-1930s when Prohibition was actively enforced. Rattner, the novel's fourteen-year-old protagonist, was abandoned as a young child by his drunkard, thieving father and was raised in poverty by his mother. Rattner is friends with an old man, Arthur Ownby, who lives in the mountains outside of the city. Ownby is an outcast and a rebel who rejects the entrapments of civilization to live alone off his land. His sole companion is his dog.

During the story, Rattner befriends a man named Marion Sylder. Sylder is in his mid-twenties. At the beginning of the story, Sylder returns to his native Knoxville like the prodigal son, flush with money, driving a new car. Readers learn that through a series of unfortunate incidents, Sylder has been pushed out of a relatively stable life as an honest working man into the life of an outlaw. Sylder has become a bootlegger. McCarthy creates him as a noble criminal whose path was altered by events beyond his control.

As the story progresses, the narrative explores John Wesley Rattner's struggle to shape a life based on his relationships with these two men. Each man represents one end of a constrained social spectrum that presents limited options for a poor, young man growing up in Prohibition-era Tennessee.

Ownby is the noble outcast who violently rejects modern society and its encroachment on his virulent independence. Sylder is a criminal who exploits society's weaknesses for his own gain and without remorse. With these two characters as his only guides, Rattner tries to figure out where he fits on the spectrum all three men share.

McCarthy constructs the story episodically. The narratives about Ownby and Sylder never overlap. The two men never meet or interact. Rattner is the link between them. Though the men do not share specific events, all three characters inhabit the same fictive world, which is driven by the same forces. For example, all three characters experience the tension between the encroachment of modern civilization and the brutal reality of life in the natural world. The minor characters in the novel articulate and amplify this clash between the diminished natural world of pastoral Appalachia and the modern world that is pushing at its borders.

As the stories of Ownby, Sylder, and Rattner become intertwined, the narrator describes the natural world they all inhabit as a place that is rife with struggle, ugliness, and decay. Nowhere is the state of this natural world more evident than in the narrative description of animals. Frogs are "gruffly choral," "pair of bitterns stalked with gimlet eyes the fertile shallows," fish are "great scaly gars ... fierce and primitive of aspect, long beaks full of teeth," and a hungry cat is "cautious, furtive, and dusted with wood-rot." All of these descriptions are from a single page of text (*The Orchard Keeper*, 173).

In this challenging environment, major and minor characters try to eke out a subsistence living by trapping small game and by bootlegging whiskey. McCarthy complicates the pastoral desire by gradually portraying this Appalachian environment and the characters that inhabit it as also being corrosive and corrupt.

Racism is not a main theme in the book, but issues of race appear throughout the narrative as a corrosive element that hinders the quest by white characters for any kind of purely pastoral existence. The main characters, Ownby, Rattner, and Sylder, do not engage in overtly hostile racist acts. However, they are part of a community that is imbued with racist elements. There is black and there is white.

For example, a minor character named Warn tells Rattner about Garland Hobie, another minor character, who is locally famous and

The idea of the warrior hero is central to the nobility with which Cormac McCarthy imbues his characters. He does this overtly. In one memorable scene, the narrator describes Ownby making his way down the side of a mountain during a raging thunderstorm. He passes a large chestnut tree just as it is struck by lighting. The force of the blast covers Ownby with "sawdust and scorched mice." The blow sends a slab of the tree hurtling at him. And then this: "He is down. A clash of shields rings and Valkyrie descend with cat's cries to bear him away" (*The Orchard Keeper*, 44). The narrator likens Ownby to a Viking warrior. That Ownby's character is noble is essential to understanding the nature of his struggle to stay on his land despite efforts by the government to move him off to make way for construction. In Norse mythology, Valkyrie are the handmaidens sent by the all-powerful god Odin to retrieve the souls of slain warriors and bring them to Valhalla, the hall where these souls are received.

infamous for shooting at some local blacks over a period of time and thus running them out of a small church they had built on the mountain. This story is merely recounted. McCarthy's characters are not interested in affecting in any way the black-white social order. They do not challenge racism, nor do they actively seek to advance it, but they do accept it. They exist as characters in a racist social order that is defined by place and time. *The Orchard Keeper,* then, lays the groundwork for the way in which McCarthy treats race in all of his Southern gothic novels. It is just there. Any judgment about the social system is imparted by the reader.

In the final half of the narrative, Arthur Ownby and Marion Sylder are incarcerated—Sylder for bootlegging and Ownby for shooting at a sheriff and wounding a deputy. John Wesley Rattner visits Ownby in what is presumably a sanatorium, and he visits Selby in jail. Rattner reveals that he has chosen his path. He wants to emulate Sylder. Rattner tries to form an allegiance with Sylder based on vengeance against the sheriff who imprisoned him. Sylder sneeringly rejects Rattner's offer.

In these incarceration scenes, Ownby and Sylder both invoke the symbolic order of the Old South, and they clearly indicate that the old social order is no longer available to any man, young or old. This latent desire to be part of the high romance of the Confederacy is evinced in

> The death of the ancient dog faintly echoes the death of Odysseus' dog, Argos, near the end of the *Odyssey*. Argos has been abused and starved by the suitors and then dies upon seeing Odysseus when he returns in disguise. The hostility toward wild and domestic animals at the end of the novel signals the emergence of a kind of epic inhospitableness toward anything human or animal.

the language of both characters. After Ownby is arrested, he condescendingly tells the social worker who is trying to help him that he talks like a Yankee. Sylder refers to his own criminal behavior of bootlegging whiskey as "blockading,'" a not-so-obscure reference to the practice of the Confederate Navy's attempts to get supplies by the Union Navy during the Civil War. These anachronisms, which emerge at the end of the narrative, serves as harbingers of each character's own lost war. Sylder and Ownby are incarcerated. Their fates are sealed; they lost.

Rattner is too young to know it yet, but his fate also is sealed. At the end of the story, Rattner returns to the county courthouse to return the one-dollar bounty that he claimed for turning in a dead hawk (at this point in history, many local governments paid bounties to people who killed predators). That particular action is simultaneously noble and futile. Rattner's innocent hostility toward modern political institutions is met with indifference by the clerk. He is searching for some kind of authentic life, but his models for manhood—Sylder and Ownby—are weak and false. More important, they are irrelevant to the modern world that John Wesley Rattner will inhabit as a man.

The tragedy of the lack of effective models in an emerging new world order is emphasized by the unhappy resolution experienced by an animal at the end of the narrative. Earlier, Arthur Ownby was tragically separated from his only friend and companion, his dog, Scout. Scout reappears at the end of the story, having somehow survived without Ownby to provide for him. As this ancient, noble beast lopes into view, he is unceremoniously shot by a cruel and small-minded police officer named Legwater. This is the world in which John Wesley Rattner must make his way, a world where cruelty and alienation have destroyed the potential for harmony.

It is in this rural, cruel, and alienated state that Cormac McCarthy sets his next novel, the unrelentingly gloomy novel *Outer Dark*.

DISCUSSION QUESTIONS

- How does McCarthy fragment the narrative of *The Orchard Keeper*?
- How does this novel draw a distinction between the antebellum South and the "new" South?
- How does McCarthy portray alienation from modern institutions?
- What is the significance of Rattner not having a father figure?
- What is the significance of the diminishment of the natural world for Arthur Ownby and for other characters?

4

OUTER DARK
(1968)

Although not a commercial success, *The Orchard Keeper* received enough critical acclaim to earn McCarthy a small audience. The book also brought grant funding to the author, which provided him with financial support while he wrote his second novel, *Outer Dark*. Page numbers cited for *Outer Dark* are from the 1993 paperback edition (New York: First Vintage International).

McCarthy composed parts of this second book while working in a writer's colony on Ibiza off the coast of Spain. Published in 1968, *Outer Dark* delves into even more unsettling psychological terrain than did his first novel. The book explicitly grapples with questions about the nature of humanity, sin, and humankind's place in the universe.

Outer Dark is a parable that addresses the timeless theme of the origin of evil. McCarthy employs violent taboos such as infanticide, incest, and cannibalism to probe human nature and sinfulness. The grotesque subject matter can be off-putting to readers and, in all likelihood, contributed to the author's relative obscurity into the early 1990s. Yet, the unswerving consideration of evil also earned him a loyal following. The environment the characters inhabit in *Outer Dark* is an extreme example of morally depravity. Yet, the novel contains elements of human compassion amid the corruption.

Outer Dark takes place somewhere in the Appalachian South. The specific locale is indeterminate, as is the historical era. This intentional obscuring of place and time differentiates the book from McCarthy's other novels and establishes the work as a timeless parable. The only clues the reader is given about setting and era are derived from the dialect, colloquialisms, and geography, all of which suggest the mountainous region of Appalachia. The setting is characterized by isolation and tremendous poverty. Like in *The Orchard Keeper*, McCarthy employs an omniscient third-person narrator and omits quotation marks from characters' speech.

From the novel's outset, McCarthy invokes biblical references: prophets abound alongside blind lepers and souls in supplication. Critics have described the setting into which Rinthy and Culla bring their inbred son as an anti-Eden. The book's title alludes to chapter 25, verse 30 from the Book of Matthew, part of the synoptic gospels in the New Testament. The verse reads: "And cast the worthless servant into the outer darkness; there men will weep and gnash their teeth." This biblical passage tells the story of a servant who, out of fear, squanders an opportunity to increase his master's wealth. The servant is punished not just because he has done something wrong, but because he has failed to do something right. Thus, he is cast into the "outer darkness," where he is condemned to suffer alone in physical and spiritual torment.

McCarthy places *Outer Dark* in an archetypal natural setting—the scenes and episodes are dominated by the forests, swamps, and small towns of rural Appalachia. These narrow settings create a fine lens through which the book explores the inherent nature of evil in the cosmos and in the human individual. The book poses two fundamental questions to readers: Did God make the world more evil than good, and why are people driven to do evil things?

To explore these aspects of evil, readers are confronted with two vicious sins in the first few pages of the book: murder and incest. The main narrative involves two adult siblings, Rinthy Holme, the sister, and her brother, Culla. Their story begins as Rinthy is about to give birth. Culla is the father of Rinthy's child. The son of Rinthy and Culla is born. Culla tells Rinthy the child is puny and that he does not expect it to live. While Rinthy sleeps after the exertions of child birth, Culla takes the infant into the woods with the intention of killing it. Instead, he abandons the child. McCarthy constructs the story as a dual narrative during which the two siblings never meet, although they encounter many of the same characters during their respective journeys. Both characters' missions end tragically.

The remainder of the story unfolds as a result of Culla's moral equivocation: his refusal to submit to an evil impulse (killing his child of incest) paradoxically brings more evil into the story. Perversely, then,

Culla is punished for not being evil enough, for he allows his sin of incest to be made public. A tinker—a nameless traveling salesman who sells hand-drawn pornography—finds the abandoned child in the woods. After the child is discovered, the baby disappears from the narrative until the end of the book.

Rinthy learns that her baby has not been buried, and she leaves the one-room cabin where the reader first encounters her to go in search of her son. Culla soon follows her. The two are never reunited. However, they traverse what is roughly the same physical trajectory through several towns. The crucial distinction between their narratives is that Culla is hunted, harassed, and almost killed everywhere he goes. Rinthy, in contrast, receives help at almost every junction and avoids disaster in spite of stumbling into dangerous conflicts. Rinthy's quest is plagued by sadness and despair, but she survives to continue her search, cloaked by the virtuous nature of her motives.

McCarthy weaves into the story a third narrative of three nameless outsiders (they are introduced on the first page of the text as "the bearded one" and "the other two") who are terrorizing the rural area through which Rinthy and Culla wander. Stylistically, McCarthy separates episodes involving these anonymous terrors from the main narrative by using italics. The italicization is a rhetorical device that establishes a philosophical distance from Rinthy and Culla and other minor characters. The violent, primal episodes involving these men are peripheral to the immediate narrative driving Rinthy and Culla. The sections involving the men initially seem to be random. But it soon becomes apparent that these outlaws are imbued with a higher purpose. They follow Culla's path, murdering people with whom he has spoken. Culla has become a harbinger of death and destruction.

One of the first characters Culla encounters on his journey in pursuit of Rinthy is a man known as the Squire. Culla works all day for this man. The next morning, Culla steals the Squire's boots and sneaks away before sunrise. Symbolically, this is a complex pastoral episode with the Squire representing the old gentrified South. Squire is a holdover term in the Appalachian South that refers to a slave-owning landowner. In the story, the Squire has a mute black man as a servant. After Culla leaves the man's estate, the Squire is killed by the three outlaws. He is dispatched violently with a brush-hook, an agrarian tool turned into a murderous weapon. Culla is blamed for the murder. In addition to being followed by the outsiders, Culla is now being pursued by the locals.

While on the run, Culla meets a walking parable in the "snake man." The snake man, who claims he would not turn even Satan away for a drink, used to earn his living hunting snakes. He hunted them all out of the area. The snake is an animal loaded with biblical symbolism. In the creation myth, the serpent brings knowledge into the world; it also led to humankind's fall from grace and expulsion from Eden. The snake man is genuinely hospitable to Culla; he is a force of good in the book. But Culla cannot remain with him because he is driven on in his quest to find Rinthy.

In Culla, McCarthy has created a character who is morally compromised (he has committed incest and contemplated infanticide), but this character also becomes the victim of circumstance, which engenders sympathy for him from the reader. Thus, Culla has a dual nature: he appears innocent and naive in spite of his moral debasement. Through Culla, McCarthy explores the limits of Christian theology by asking the reader to forgive even the most horrible acts.

The nature of the next two episodes suggests that McCarthy is interested in showing how Christianity is insufficient in understanding the nature of evil. The first episode alludes to the Book of Matthew (8:28–34). Culla is falsely accused of letting a pig stampede carry off one of its drovers. What ensues is a darkly gross and comic episode in which one of the drovers, who is a "preacher," decides, along with the rest of the group, that Culla should be hung. The group readily assents. They decide to hang him because one member of the group "ain't never seen no one hung before" (*Outer Dark*, 224). After more deliberation, the mob decides to "flang" him off the cliff into the river. Culla escapes.

The related passage from the Book of Matthew recounts the story of Jesus coming to a town after crossing a lake by boat. When he steps foot

Passage 8:28–34 from the Book of Matthew reads: (28) When he arrived at the other side in the region of the Gadarenes, two demon-possessed men coming from the tombs met him. They were so violent that no one could pass that way. (29) "What do you want with us, Son of God?" they shouted. "Have you come here to torture us before the appointed time?" (30) Some distance from them a large herd of pigs was feeding. (31) The demons begged Jesus, "If you drive us out, send us into the herd of pigs." (32) He said to them, "Go!" So they came out and went into the pigs, and the whole herd rushed down the steep bank into the lake and died in the water. (33) Those tending the pigs ran off, went into the town and reported all this, including what had happened to the demon-possessed men. (34) Then the whole town went out to meet Jesus. And when they saw him, they pleaded with him to leave their region. (*New American Bible*) on land, two men, possessed by demons, run up to him and demand to know why Jesus is there. They ask if he is there to torture them "before the appointed time" (8:29). The demons then beg Jesus to drive them out into a herd of grazing pigs. Jesus commands them to go, and the demons are driven into the herd and carried down a steep hill into the lake, where the herd drowns. The townspeople who witnessed the event then plead with Jesus to leave.

In this episode, McCarthy is toying with the Christian idea of evil by re-imagining the passage from the Book of Matthew. Although Culla, who is pretty far down on the scale of human sinfulness, is falsely accused of sending the pig drover to his death, this is not the sin Culla has committed. This perversion of justice suggests that a higher moral order is at work in the world, but one that operates through human beings in unknown and convoluted ways.

As Culla is pursued by the townspeople seeking vengeance for the death of the pig drover, the novel descends even further into its exploration of the nature of evil when Culla meets the three nameless outsiders. The men somehow have come into possession of the baby that Culla and Rinthy have been hunting. The episode that follows is one of the more unsettling passages in all of McCarthy's work. In it, Culla is forced by the leader of the three men to eat some kind of meat that is probably human. It gets worse. Culla then sees his son's throat cut by one of the unnamed men who drinks its blood and then eats the child. This instance of cannibalism and infanticide is a perverse punishment for Culla's sins. Inexplicably, the three men release Culla after taking his boots.

The novel concludes with two enduring images. Culla meets a blind man and does not steer the blind man away from a road that leads into a swamp. Culla thus appears doomed to bear his sin forever. Rinthy discovers the hanging body of the tinker along with the tiny bones of what remains of her son in the camp where the three men harassed Culla.

The biblical allusions in the book juxtaposed with the taboos of murder, infanticide, and cannibalism leave a profoundly dark vision of humanity's origins and destiny. This darkness coalesces even more sharply in the main protagonist, Lester Ballard, whose impulses drive the narrative of McCarthy's next novel, *Child of God*.

DISCUSSION QUESTIONS

- How does McCarthy use the Bible in this novel?
- Why do the three men not kill Culla?

- What taboos does McCarthy explore in this novel?
- How does McCarthy portray the natural world?
- What is the significance of the Squire's title?
- What examples of the Southern gothic literary tradition are present in this novel?
- Why does McCarthy italicize the passages in which the three unnamed men appear?

5

CHILD OF GOD
(1973)

Child of God, published in 1973, continues McCarthy's examination of the nature of evil and human sinfulness as expressed through moral depravity and the grotesque violation of social taboos. The story immerses readers in some of the same unsettling terrain from McCarthy's previous novels in which acts of human degeneracy drive the narrative—thievery, incest, rape, and murder. There is one main difference: the protagonist in *Child of God* devolves into the most debased and corrupt main character in all of McCarthy's works to date. Page numbers cited from *Child of God* are from the 1993 paperback edition (New York: First Vintage International).

The story is set in a place called Sevier County (an echo of Sevierville from *The Orchard Keeper*). Like *Outer Dark,* the location of the action vacillates between scenes in town and scenes in wild nature, which feature mountains, caves, and abandoned houses. Poverty abounds.

The narrative chronicles the rapid descent of Lester Ballard from social outcast to deranged serial killer and necrophiliac. The book opens with a dramatic scene of an adult Ballard being driven out of his home. The county has claimed Ballard's farm, and auctioneers and townspeople have poured onto his land to bid for his property. As the auction begins, Ballard refuses to leave and becomes agitated, hostile, and aggressive. Then, he is blindsided by a man named "Buster," who hits Ballard in the head with an ax with such force that blood streams out of both Ballard's ears.

The narrative techniques McCarthy uses to tell the story vary somewhat from the omniscient third-person narrator of his earlier works. The opening auction scene is told by a nameless insider who knows Ballard and the other characters who populate the story. The narrator speaks in the local dialect and employs first-person storytelling devices like narrative asides. These asides suggest that Ballard's story is being told at some point in time after the story's action has been resolved. Describing what happens to Ballard after he was struck with the ax, the narrator says, "Lester Ballard never could hold his head right after that. It must of thowed [sic] his neck out someway or another" (*Child of God*, 9).

This nameless local drops in and out of the first of the book's three sections to share insider information about Ballard's past and present. He says, "I was raised with him [Ballard] over in the tenth. I was ahead of him in school" (*Child of God*, 17). Ballard's contemporary recounts how, as an adult, Ballard summoned him and another man to cut down Ballard's father after he hung himself in his barn. And then, at the end of the section, the narrator reveals that he was sitting around with a group of other men telling stories about Ballard. He disappears from the novel after saying he has to go home to get his supper.

The majority of the narrative is conveyed through an omniscient third-person voice that is similar to the one that populates McCarthy's earlier works. The voice is articulate and detached and uses clear, concise, descriptive language.

The picture of Ballard that emerges from the narrative as a whole is of a man who both rejects and has been rejected by contemporary society. As a youth, he was disliked by his peers for his unprovoked violence and aggression. As an adult, "he'd grown lean and bitter. Some said mad. A malign star kept him" (*Child of God*, 41). He scrapes a meager existence off the land. He peddles stolen property for petty cash. He lives alone in a rotting, abandoned house in the woods. The only person with whom he socializes is the drunken patriarch of a junkyard who lords over his brood of promiscuous, inebriated daughters.

Anne DeLisle speaks about McCarthy's penchant for showering after writing. It was during their time together in Tennessee that McCarthy wrote *Child of God*. She claims that it was as though McCarthy had to "wash" all of this horrible stuff off of him. After his shower, he would say that it was time for a "cocktail."

McCarthy portrays Ballard as a solitary, primitive creature driven by his own elemental needs. Ballard's psychology remains obscure to the reader throughout the novel; only his actions are portrayed with clarity. His sole talent is superior marksmanship, which he displays at a county fair when he wins a near-impossible target-shooting game. He is rewarded with three gigantic stuffed animals, and then the pitchman for the game cuts him off. This is the only episode in the story in which Ballard experiences a triumph, but it is a fleeting and profoundly solitary victory.

After this episode, Ballard's life goes from bad to worse. He is falsely accused of rape and imprisoned for three days. After his release, he's out hunting for squirrels when he stumbles across a dead couple in a parked car on the side of a mountain road. The car is running. The couple has been asphyxiated. Ballard takes the body of the dead woman to his decrepit house, where he keeps her as his lover.

Ballard goes into town to buy clothing and lingerie for this dead captive. When he returns to his house in the mountains, he dresses the woman up and seats her at his dining table. In a scene of desperate but morbid poignancy, Ballard goes outside and looks at her through the window. This powerful and melancholy instance of voyeurism displays Ballard's desire to be normal. He is imagining a regular life that he has never and will never have. After this romantic fantasy, Ballard's house catches fire and burns to the ground. He is displaced, the corpse is incinerated, and he seeks refuge in a cave.

Thus begins his descent into total madness. After the loss of the corpse in the fire, he devolves into a psychotic serial killer and necrophiliac. He stores the bodies of his female victims in a chamber of the underground caverns that are now his home. His madness eventually gets the better of him, and in a bizarre scene, he emerges from his cave, dressed in the clothing of one of his victims, and shoots the man who, in all probability, bought Ballard's house from the sheriff's auction. Ballard loses an arm in the ensuing gunfight, is jailed, escapes temporarily, and staggers to the county hospital where he turns himself in. He spends the rest of his days in a sanatorium.

Ballard's actions challenge the conventional novelistic device of creating a protagonist with whom the reader seeks to identify on some level. In spite of Ballard's repugnant character, McCarthy weaves a story that allows the reader to feel pity for this man-become-monster. Ballard is a true anti-hero. From the beginning of the novel, he is at odds with society.

McCarthy cultivates the reader's sympathy for Ballard by linking his plight with our own. The omniscient narrator addresses the reader and

First editions of this novel sell for as much as $1,500, according to http://www.abebooks.com.

says, "You could say that he's sustained by his fellow men, like you. Has peopled the shore with them calling to him. A race that gives suck to the maimed and the crazed, that wants their wrong blood in their history and will have it" (*Child of God*, 156). Ballard thus becomes anointed as a member of the common human experience. He is cast here by the narrator not as an outsider but as an outlaw who makes up part of the human narrative. He is one of us.

The novel concludes with a ghoulish description of an autopsy being performed by the state on Ballard's remains. McCarthy calls the four doctors conducting the autopsy *haruspices*: an archaic word for people who used to tell the future by reading entrails. By invoking this ancient rite, McCarthy positions the story of Lester Ballard as one of many on a continuum of horrible tales about the darker aspects of human nature. It is a sad and ghoulish end to a sad and ghoulish life. But it is not the worst life of all. In Ballard's entrails, the doctors "perhaps saw monsters worse to come in their configurations" (*Child of God*, 194).

McCarthy abandons this universal pessimism for the highly idiosyncratic and autobiographical narrative in McCarthy's next novel, *Suttree*, which supposedly took him more than twenty years to write.

DISCUSSION QUESTIONS

- Compare the use of the Southern gothic genre in *Child of God* to *Outer Dark*.
- What is the significance of Lester's talent for shooting?
- How does Lester's traumatic family background influence his psychology?
- What taboos does McCarthy explore in this novel?
- How does McCarthy's narrative in this novel differ from *The Orchard Keeper*?
- Why does McCarthy call Lester a child of God?
- What is a haruspice?

6

SUTTREE
(1979)

Set in 1950s Knoxville, the novel *Suttree* follows the escapades, tragic and comic, of Cornelius Suttree, a ne'er-do-well son of a prominent family from Knoxville, Tennessee. The novel follows Cornelius Suttree through a variety of episodes that involve drinking, fighting, fishing, labor, imprisonment, hospitalization, petty thievery, sexual escapades, family fights, and, ultimately, his departure from the McAnally Flats neighborhood of Knoxville. Suttree survives by eating and selling fish that he catches in the Tennessee River. The novel features a series of episodes during which Suttree interacts with various groups and individuals from Knoxville's black and white underclass. Page numbers cited for *Suttree* are from the 1992 paperback edition (New York: First Vintage International).

McCarthy employs the same minimalist treatment of dialogue in *Suttree* that he used in his previous books—he omits quotation marks. And like his earlier works, *Suttree* features an omniscient third-person narrator who is prone to evocative, lengthy descriptions. In fact, *Suttree*, which was published in 1979, is written in the traditional mode of social realism but with an encyclopedic and epic scope. One classic characteristic of the epic genre is that it represents "the known world." McCarthy's novel attempts this feat. *Suttree* also features a comic rather than a tragic arc, which differentiates it from McCarthy's previous novels and

In Knoxville, there is a pub-crawl known as the Suttree Stagger, which celebrates the novel and follows some of the actual haunts of Suttree that still exist in Knoxville. For further detail about the actual physical background of Suttree, there is a fascinating link on the Cormac McCarthy Society Web site called *Searching for Suttree*. This detailed Web page has mapped all the salient locations that are named in the novel. This local detail is part of the charm of the novel, yet it is not at all a bar to the general reader.

from almost all of his successive novels. (The term comic refers to the classic literary definition and defines stories in which the protagonist successfully overcomes obstacles instead of being overcome by those obstacles.) In these ways, this text differs substantially from his first three novels.

Suttree is McCarthy's farewell homage to alcoholism in Knoxville, Tennessee. As expansive as the book is, almost everything that happens to Suttree, and in particular his homelessness, can be tied to alcohol. Suttree has chosen to live a Spartan life as a fisherman in his fishing boat, so that he can pursue his drinking in a manner that is free from other distractions such as work and relationships. Set against this alcoholic pastoral is a huge cast of secondary characters in which Suttree becomes more and more alienated from himself, society, and his family. What makes the narrative so engaging is that McCarthy slows the frenetic pace of the narrative that characterizes his first three novels. The novel creates a tremendously detailed and nuanced feel for Suttree as a character and for Knoxville as a place. The novel has pathos that has been missing in his work up to this point.

Suttree opens with an esoteric narrative passage set in italics. The unidentified narrator functions like the chorus does in epic Greek dramas, by setting the stage on which the story will unfold using an omniscient, stream-of-consciousness narrative perspective. This is one of McCarthy's overt nods to one of Faulkner's hallmark techniques. McCarthy used this stage-setting approach in previous novels (*Child of God* and *Outer Dark*, for example). But in *Suttree*, the sentences in this opening passage oscillate between being overtly lyric and short and punchy. After setting the stage, this narrator disappears.

For the course of the novel McCarthy presents the world to his readers in the mind and actions of Cornelius Suttree. Suttree, the "reprobate scion," inhabits a simultaneous gothic and comic atmosphere. The poverty, drinking, and homelessness provide the gothic sensibility, and the astounding array of characters and drinking provide some comic elements.

Class tension is what has severed Suttree from his father, and Suttree is the classic fallen son. In one of the book's first scenes, Suttree's maternal uncle, John, visits Suttree's shanty on the water. Suttree tells John that his father always expected him (Suttree) to turn out badly because his father "married beneath him." In a scene rife with tension, Suttree tells his uncle that "When a man marries beneath him, his children are beneath him.... As it is, my case was always doubtful. I was expected to turn out badly.... My grandfather used to say Blood will tell" (*Suttree*, 19). Suttree continues to berate his uncle, telling him that, to his father, his mother is a mere housekeeper and that his father "probably believes that only his own benevolent guidance kept her out of the whorehouse" (*Suttree*, 20).

When the novel opens, Suttree is living up to his grandfather's prophecy. He is fresh out of the workhouse (a step below full-blown prison) and lives alone, barely scraping an existence out of the river on which his house floats. The novel follows Suttree out of one episode and into the next as he stumbles from one drunken bender to another.

The novel is McCarthy's most racially diverse. Racial antagonism is present between Knoxville police and Knoxville blacks. Suttree, however, inhabits a drunken racial Utopia in which he peacefully coexists with blacks. For Suttree, drink breaches any racial divide. In one memorable scene, he shares a meal with a Native American. After a vivid scene in which he skins a large snapping turtle, the man cooks Suttree a dish of turtle soup. Suttree's contribution to the meal is beer.

In *Suttree*, McCarthy employs several of the mainstay themes of the Southern gothic genre. One of those is the character of the imbecile, in this novel named Gene Harrogate. Of the numerous characters that populate this tome, Harrogate is one of the novel's more memorable. He meets Suttree in the workhouse, where both men have been consigned. Harrogate has been arrested for sodomizing watermelons. He is a savant petty criminal in the mold of Lester Ballard but without the murderous tendencies. Suttree is sympathetic to the plight of Harrogate—he knows that Harrogate will never fit into society, whereas he himself has chosen not to fit in. Harrogate ultimately takes up residence in a cave under one of Knoxville's bridges.

This particular universe that McCarthy creates in the novel shows that Suttree is at home in a variety of physical places and by extension in all of the strata of Knoxville's underclass. Suttree appears in the backrooms of bars, on his boat, in the black section of Knoxville, in prison, isolated in a hotel room with the delirium tremens, in a hospital near death, and camped out with a family of itinerant pearl dredgers upriver from Knoxville. Suttree falls in love with one of the daughters of the pearl dredgers, but, unsurprisingly perhaps, that relationship quickly and fatally comes to an end.

Unlike McCarthy's main characters that preceded him, Suttree is liked by nearly everyone with whom he comes in contact. He lives a life of poverty; yet, he has a sense of belonging that none of McCarthy's other characters have. In only one instance in the novel is Suttree unlikable. Suttree impregnates a young woman and will not marry her. He is then attacked by the girl's mother and subsequently forced to leave Knoxville by a local sheriff, who gives him a bus ticket. Suttree has been exiled. He ends up in a small town in North Carolina, barely able to walk. Suttree orders a meal for himself in a restaurant and is unable to eat, so he goes outside and wanders the streets until he decides to take another bus back to Knoxville.

This return to Knoxville marks the final scenes in the novel's picaresque drama. Suttree is back in town drinking at a bar when he allows himself to be picked up by one of two prostitutes, a woman named Joyce. In the ensuing episodes with Joyce, Suttree is strangely passive. He allows her to keep him in a hotel room and accepts lots of money from her. Accepting money from other people is out of character for Suttree, who repaid an uncle several months after borrowing a mere $20 from him. Suttree has jettisoned his personal code of independence and chosen to hand himself over to Joyce's control. They do enjoy themselves together—she likes his good looks, he likes their physical relationship, and they bond over drinking and getting quite drunk. The relationship finally gives way, and in a rage she tries kicking out the window of a car they have purchased together. Suttree coolly explains the situation to a police officer, and he is allowed to leave the scene without being arrested. After the fight in the car, Suttree hallucinates violently, vomits, and is stranded alone inside a hotel room.

Near death, he is somehow miraculously discovered by one of his drinking buddies, J-Bone, who takes him to a hospital, where they put Suttree in the old people's ward with indigent and elderly who are dying. In his diseased, weakened, and demented state, Suttree clings to life. The

Many residents of Knoxville are said to have read the novel in great detail to find themselves in it. Of his days in Knoxville, McCarthy has said that the people he drank with are either dead or have stopped drinking. McCarthy has a brother, a lawyer, who still lives in Knoxville.

> The striking hallucinatory passages in *Suttree* might be attributed to the fact that McCarthy took acid. However, he took it before it became illegal. Garry Wallace describes this in his 1992 essay in *Southern Quarterly*, "Meeting McCarthy."

passages that McCarthy devotes to the hallucinations in the hotel room and in the hospital are powerful, disturbing, and in retrospect somewhat elegiac as they signal the end to a certain kind of life for Suttree and for Knoxville itself.

As Suttree leaves Knoxville for god-knows-where in a cab, McAnally Flats is being razed to modernize the downtown area. His flight without goodbyes to any of his family or friends echoes the fierce, stoic, and romantic independence of his departure from the family of pearl dredgers. In that departure, McCarthy wrote that Suttree was determined to tell no man or soul what he had seen or what he had done. In Suttree's tragic isolation at the conclusion of the novel, there is a faint glimmer of optimism in his mere survival. But even more than that, there is the sense that Suttree has done something heroic in extricating himself from the darkly romantic, yet undeniably toxic, life of Knoxville's underclass.

In the twofold rejection of the drinking life and the repudiation of Knoxville, McCarthy abandons the Southern pastoral, an ideology that has not existed in the real world for at least one hundred years. He also abandons the South itself as a source for more books. Consequently, we can see these thematic and narrative moves as McCarthy moves away from Faulkner and toward another arena of American literature, the West.

As dark as *Suttree* was, his next book, *Blood Meridian*, would prove to be far darker than anything McCarthy had previously imagined.

DISCUSSION QUESTIONS

- How is *Suttree* an encyclopedic novel?
- What is the significance of alcohol in the novel?
- Why does Suttree flee McAnally Flats?
- Why does he not want to be with his family?
- Why does Suttree call Catholicism "Christian Witchcraft"?
- How is Suttree dissimilar from other protagonists in McCarthy novels?

- How is the narrative of *Suttree* different from other McCarthy novels?
- Why do you think it took McCarthy almost twenty years to write *Suttree*?
- How does McCarthy represent poverty?
- How does McCarthy represent friendship in the novel?

7

BLOOD MERIDIAN
(1985)

Set primarily along the Texas-Mexico border in the mid-nineteenth century, *Blood Meridian* is one of McCarthy's most well-known novels. (The book's full title is *Blood Meridian: Or the Evening Redness in the West*, but it is commonly referred to simply as *Blood Meridian*.) It is a coming-of-age story that takes place during the brutal epoch of Westward expansion in American history. Page numbers cited for *Blood Meridian* are from the 1992 paperback edition (New York: First Vintage International).

The book begins with three epigraphs. The first two are from historic intellectual figures—the Frenchman Paul Valéry, whose writings spanned the late nineteenth and early twentieth century, and a German, Jacob Boehme, who lived during the mid-sixteenth and early seventeenth centuries. The third epigraph is from a contemporary newspaper story. The epigraphs set the stage for the book's main themes: a condemnation of mindless acts of cruelty, a comment on the nature of the "life of darkness," and a snippet about the history of scalping. The grim epigraphs portend the violence and bloodshed in the novel.

The story opens with an omniscient narrative voice that McCarthy used in his Southern gothic works. Again, like the chorus in a classical epic, the narrator sets the story's stage using language that swings between lyrical, almost antiquated phrases, and short direct sentences:

McCarthy received grant funding from three different foundations to write *Blood Meridian*: the Lyndhurst Foundation, the John Simon Guggenheim Memorial Foundation, and the Catherine T. MacArthur Foundation. With the grant monies, he conducted extensive historical research. This book, then, represents a convergence of McCarthy's talent as a writer and his significant intellect. The epigraphs he includes at the beginning of the novel illustrate that union.

"his folks are known for hewers of wood and drawers of water but in truth his father has been a schoolmaster. He lies in drink, he quotes from poets whose names are now lost" (*Blood Meridian*, 3).

This narrator describes the origins of the story's protagonist, a nameless young man, known only as "the kid," who was born in 1833 and runs away from home at age fourteen. The kid is somewhere in Tennessee when he "wanders west as far as Memphis." Over the course of two years, he wends his way through a series of treacherous events from St. Louis to New Orleans to Texas. In 1849, he lands in Fredonia, a region in present-day Texas that had been the site of a land battle between the Mexican government and the would-be founders of a separatist republic. Texas had been annexed by the U.S. government in 1845, and by 1849, the region was a hotbed of competing interests among the Mexican government, Native Americans, the U.S. government, and Texas republicans. The landgrab spawned brutal violence and ceaseless conflict.

The kid joins the army under the leadership of a Captain White. Captain White is in the service of the U.S. Army and is waging war against Mexico to enable "Americans ... to get to California without having to pass through our benighted sister republic and our citizens will be protected at last from the notorious packs of cutthroats presently infesting the routes which they are obliged to travel" (*Blood Meridian*, 34). White believes his mission to be noble, just, and sanctioned by the Monroe Doctrine. The kid joins the army, and while riding out to California, the entire expedition is massacred by a band of Comanches. The kid is one of a handful of survivors.

After this baptism by bloodbath, the kid is captured and sent to jail in Mexico. By a twist of fate, he is picked up by a band of mercenary Indian hunters. The posse is paid by the governor of the Mexican province of Chihuahua for every Indian scalp they bring. The last three-fourths of the story describe in violent detail bloody and cruel scalp-hunting episodes. The narrative concludes with the kid, now in his mid-30s, wandering alone around California, where he has a mysterious and fatal encounter that concludes this terrifying story of Westward expansion.

Like *Moby Dick*, the book that inspired its vision and scope—McCarthy says that it is one of his favorite books—*Blood Meridian* begins with a three-word sentence: "See the child." But instead of Ishmael's subjective narration, readers of McCarthy's book are instantly called to bear witness to something—the horrific elements of Westward expansion that repudiate benign versions of American history. While McCarthy is writing a distinctly American novel, he is also writing about the inherently ignoble nature of war. The novel clearly has cosmic aims—as evinced by the opening epigraphs that frame the novel's philosophical exploration of war and violence in as large a historical context as possible.

Blood Meridian is also a transitional novel in that it begins in Tennessee and moves to the American Southwest. Its nihilistic content is offset by an unmatched lyrical and epic prosody that has inspired both critical admiration and revulsion. McCarthy's beautiful prose contrasts the grotesqueries of war in a way that forces readers to question their sentimental relationship with the way that literature renders brutal realities as literary abstractions. Furthermore, McCarthy strips away all romanticism from the practice of war to make readers realize that war is always about killing. The central paradox of this war novel is that the protagonists, the scalp hunters, avoid confrontations in which they would be outnumbered. Instead, they ply their paramilitary trade in that infamous form that characterized a lot of conflict in the American West, the massacre.

In constructing massacre after massacre, McCarthy tracks the assemblage, ascendance, and destruction of a band of scalp hunters led primarily by two men, Judge Holden and John Joel Glanton. The Judge is a mythic creature, much like Melville's white whale. He is a seven-foot, hairless albino with a powerful intellect. He is fluent in many languages and has a comprehensive knowledge of history, science, religion, and philosophy. He is a human embodiment of the white whale itself. He is also a grotesque manifestation of the "whiteness" that will forever be linked to the genocidal aspects of Westward expansion. Together, the Judge and Glanton form an erudite and completely pitiless force against not only any Indians but anyone who thwarts them in their pursuit of scalps. Their tremendous violence seems almost hyperbolic; however, both men are based on historical characters. This use of actual characters suggests another primary aim of McCarthy's: the demythologizing of a benign Westward expansion as part of America's self-definition.

Of equal importance to the Judge and Glanton is McCarthy's unnamed protagonist, the kid. His name connotes much about the ways in which Americans and the larger world have mythologized the West by

Interestingly, a minor but famous aspect of the novel's publishing history centers around Joseph Sepich's book, *Notes on Blood Meridian*, in which he identifies many of the primary sources that give the novel its historical authenticity. While Sepich's finely researched book was out of print (it was reissued in 2008), in the rare book market it commanded a price almost as high as some first editions of the novel itself. This secondary source on the novel was of critical importance in that it supplied early critics of McCarthy with some much-needed foundational information. For example, the surreal episode that features babies impaled on the branches of a tree by Indians would appear fantastical, yet it has a historical basis in fact. This minor yet powerful example shows how war is all encompassing and illuminates the enduring reality that in a time of all-out war, even innocents are viewed as combatants.

associating it with innocence, youth, vitality, and individualism. McCarthy pulverizes that myth by immersing the kid in the murderous aesthetic of Glanton and the Judge. The kid does retain some small bit of humanity, which allows him to reemerge as an important narrative presence at the end of the book. Like Melville's Ishmael, the kid is essential to the narrative at the beginning and the end of the novel, but he is felt as an absence in the middle of the book. The kid's disappearance enables the development of the novel's epic scope.

As *Suttree* is an encyclopedic novel about the environs of Knoxville, *Blood Meridian,* with its overwhelming presentation of historical arcana that ranges from Gnosticism, to the tarot, to the recipe for making gunpowder using human urine, is an epic novel about war as being the ultimate state of human existence. Thus we see McCarthy exposing what he sees underlying the pastoral ideology, the desire to kill. Nowhere is this more clearly stated than in the disturbing inscription on the Judge's rifle, *Et in Arcadia Ego.* The loose translation is "And I am also in Arcadia." Arcadia is the original locale of the pastoral life for the Greeks. This Latin allusion to the eternal presence or threat of violence is a part of the novel's allusive aesthetic and also shows another stage in the development of McCarthy's interest in the American pastoral.

The story ends with the band of scalp hunters being pursued into oblivion by the Yuma Indian Tribe. Only a few members survive. In the end, the scalp hunters fight each other to survive the harsh desert environment. At stake is the kid's revolver, a Whitneyville Colt, of which each man in the scalp hunter band originally had two. Now, out of the whole band, only the kid has one left. The kid and a former priest, a man named Tobin, are in flight from the Judge, after the kid refused to sell the Judge his weapon. In this concluding action, the kid and Tobin fight a duel with the Judge in the open plains of the desert. The ex-priest is shot in the neck, and the kid escapes from the murderous and satanic Judge. Years later, when the kid is around forty, the Judge kills him in an outhouse. But readers never bear witness to Tobin's death. The uncertainty of Tobin's survival is the only unresolved aspect of McCarthy's nihilistic narrative.

Before the duel, two minor characters, Toadvine and David Brown meet the Judge in the desert. The Judge buys a hat and a rifle from them, but at the end of the book, readers learn that both men are hanged. Thus, the only survivors at the end of the book are the Judge—McCarthy's demonic incarnation of war itself—and the kid. However, it is plausible that Tobin also has survived. For Tobin, who has raped, sodomized, and murdered his way through the entire narrative, the Judge has been a brutally corrupting force. A poignant scene at the end of the novel suggests Tobin's repentance. When he and the kid are trying to kill the Judge, Tobin realizes the hopelessness of the situation. He lashes together some sheep bones in the form of a cross and advances upon the Judge reciting Latin. In all of McCarthy's works, this representation of Tobin may be the only substantial time when a character actually invokes Christ. In addition, sheep are heavily imbued with biblical symbolism. The ex-priest confronts the Judge using symbols of innocence and purity.

All epics have well-developed female characters and an important female presence. Despite *Blood Meridian*'s epic strivings, the lack of a significant female presence is one of the book's Achilles' heels. Therefore, McCarthy's novel is not universal: for good or ill, it is a distinctive philosophy that is relevant to men. What is interesting is that his next novel, *All the Pretty Horses*, features his two most thoroughly developed female characters in all of his novels. In fact, the gulf between the subject matter of *Blood Meridian* and *All the Pretty Horses* is so wide that it raises the question, "Is *All the Pretty Horses* McCarthy's overture written intentionally for women?"

DISCUSSION QUESTIONS

- Why does the kid disappear from the narrative?
- What is the significance of the multicultural nature of the scalp hunters?

- Why doesn't the kid shoot the Judge?
- Does Tobin, the ex-priest, survive his wounds?
- Why does the Judge claim that "War is God."
- How does *Blood Meridian* work against stereotypical ideas about the West?
- Why does the Judge kill the kid?
- What is the Judge wearing when he meets the kid in the desert?
- How does the encyclopedic nature of *Blood Meridian* differ from *Suttree?*
- How does the novel function as a philosophical exploration of violence?

8

ALL THE PRETTY HORSES
(1992)

All the Pretty Horses is a modern Western about two young men who, in the face of a dying ranching industry in the contemporary Southwest, decide to abandon their homes and families to seek their fortunes in Mexico. Page numbers cited for *All the Pretty Horses* are from the 1993 paperback edition (New York: First Vintage International).

Set in West Texas in the year 1948, the book opens as the main character, sixteen-year-old John Grady Cole, struggles to adapt to changing social circumstances within the context of a disappearing American West. The family ranch has been sold, which leaves him bereft of his future. In the wake of this news, Cole and his best friend, Lacey Rawlins, steal away from their hometown on horseback. Their plan is to ride into Mexico and hire themselves out as ranch hands to one of the still thriving cattle ranches south of the border.

Cole and Rawlins have several minor adventures as they make their way through Mexico's border country before they are hired to work on the ranch of a wealthy Mexican landowner. There on the Mexican ranch, Cole displays his prodigious talent for breaking wild horses. His expertise brings him renown. It also attracts the attention of the *hacendado*'s daughter, Alejandra, with whom he falls in love. The rest of the story follows the tragic arc of the dissolution of their love affair, and

All the Pretty Horses won the National Book Award in 1992. While it is an accomplished novel, many critics feel that this award was given to compensate for the lack of attention that *Blood Meridian* received.

Cole's subsequent return to Mexico in a final, ill-fated attempt to win back his former lover.

Published on the heels of the dark, bloody, and apocalyptic *Blood Meridian*, the content of *All the Pretty Horses* surprised McCarthy's small but loyal following of readers. The latter book was a radical shift from the author's gothic aesthetic. *All the Pretty Horses* is linked thematically to *Blood Meridian* in that both are Westerns. Both books feature young male protagonists who go off in search of their fortunes. Both books explore the theme of a disappearing Western frontier, though from distinctly different perspectives. But there are few other similarities between *Horses* and McCarthy's earlier work.

All the Pretty Horses functions as a melancholy homage to the disappearing cliché of the American cowboy. The landscape is lovingly described. Unlike the anonymous, joyless kid in *Blood Meridian* whose quest is constrained by the need to survive, the main characters in *Horses*, Cole and Rawlins, are more fully developed. Their decision to run away is not at all menacing, unlike the drivers of action in McCarthy's previous books. It is the gentle whim of hope-filled youth in search of a dream.

But from the book's beginning, it is apparent that the pursuit of the dream of living as a rancher in America is a futile anachronism. Cole's parents are separated and have not lived together in more than six years. Cole's grandfather has died, leaving the family ranch to Cole's mother, an aspiring actress. She says the ranch hasn't been profitable in more than twenty years, and days after her father's death, she sells the property. The sale is made only after she has convinced her estranged husband to sign over any claim to the land. Cole's father is a veteran of World War II and a gambler. His biggest gambling haul was $26,000 over twenty-two hours of play, but at the start of the story, he is down on his luck and ailing and is of no assistance to Cole in his attempt to keep the property. After his dad abandons his hopes and failing to convince his mother that he can run the ranch, Cole and his friend, Lacey Rawlins, saddle their horses and ride away.

Cole's desire to go to Mexico is more complicated than the urge to escape from the depressing fact of losing his ranch. As the story opens, the reader learns that John Grady Cole has a Mexican grandmother in his family tree, and in this mixed racial history, Cole's is a quintessentially American quest to explore his roots.

The character of John Grady Cole is another self-sufficient savant who inhabits the beautiful and melancholy margins of society. Cole has prodigal, mythical skills with horses. He loves the animals passionately and unconditionally. The narrative develops around Cole's character and his relationship with horses. During one of the minor adventures that precede his arrival at the Mexican ranch, he and Rawlins randomly encounter a young boy named Jimmy Blevins, who is somewhere around the age of thirteen. Blevins is riding a magnificent prize horse, one which is incredibly valuable and one which Blevins obviously has stolen. Blevins's stolen horses become a lynchpin to the story.

In the meantime, Cole's prodigious talents lead him to an important position at a ranch in Mexico called *La Hacienda de Nuestra Señora de la Purísima Concepción*, where he and Lacey find work as cowboys. They are both profoundly happy with their new positions, and on the first night at the ranch agree that they could stay down in Mexico for a hundred years. Yet, as beautiful as their life is, things quickly change for them when John Grady Cole meets the willful and beautiful daughter of Don Hector Rocha y Villareal, the *hacendado* of the ranch.

In this Western *bildungsroman*, McCarthy branches out into uncharted thematic territory for the author—male and female romance. Many critics and readers have wondered why he does not write about this subject matter in other novels, because the love affair between John and Alejandra is poignantly and powerfully rendered. McCarthy captures the excitement, risk, and doom of their relationship in a way that adds depth to the tragic dimension of this Western. Usually, McCarthy's male characters are not seeking to become permanently attached to a woman, but Cole falls so deeply in love with Alejandra that the strength of his emotion imbues him with wisdom, sadness, and a willingness to die.

Cole and Alejandra's beautiful and passionate affair is short-lived. Her father discovers their relationship and is enraged. His fury is stoked by his knowledge that Cole is somehow connected to Jimmy Blevins. By this point in the story, Blevins has become an outlaw. Blevins is like

---

The book's title comes from a child's lullaby. This traditional lullaby emphasizes John Grady Cole's loss of innocence. "When you wake you shall have/all the pretty little horses" are the essential lines that show the disparity between John's desires and what he actually attains. The novel's title excludes the word "little."

many of McCarthy's male characters in that he is wildly flawed but in some way gifted. His talent is shooting. After a series of mishaps, Blevins shoots a Mexican police officer. At the time, he was seen riding with two other gringos—Rawlins and Cole—and he's being hunted, as are the men who were seen riding with him. After the shooting, Cole and Rawlins go to work for the Mexican ranch. Blevins strikes out on his own. The Mexican police eventually track down Cole and Rawlins at Alejandra's ranch, and they arrest the two young men. After almost securing his pastoral ideal by taming wild horses on the *hacendado*'s property, Cole's dream comes to an abrupt end when Alejandra's father turns him and Rawlins over to the Mexican authorities. The reader is left to wonder whether Alejandra's father would have permitted the relationship to flourish had Cole not been associated with Blevins.

Cole, Rawlins, and Blevins are taken together to a Mexican penitentiary. Along the way, a relative of the man Blevins shoots seeks his revenge. The traumatic episode is a harbinger of the horror the young men will experience in the Mexican jail where they are subject to brutal attacks by other prisoners. This fighting culminates in a dramatic knife fight. John Grady Cole barely escapes with his life. After spending several days in a dark room, he and Rawlins are inexplicably released from prison. Upon their release, they part ways—Cole to the ranch and Rawlins back home to Texas. As the two good friends go their separate ways, Cole's character has lost two of the three guiding forces in his life: ranching and friendship. All that is left is his love for Alejandra.

In short order, Cole is stripped of romantic love. This happens over the course of several dramatic scenes. The first features Cole locked in a chess match with Alejandra's formidable aunt. Cole prevails, but during the game, he learns that he was released from prison because the aunt bought his freedom on the condition that Alejandra never see him again. Cole tells the aunt she had no right to do such a thing and that she should have let him die in jail. Cole's romantic gesture is noble, but there is a growing awareness of the futility of his simplistic view of love in a complicated world.

Cole persuades Alejandra to meet him in Mexico City, and in the course of their meeting, Alejandra ultimately rejects him. An embittered Cole leaves Alejandra to seek vengeance on the man responsible for the brutal treatment he received in prison. Cole then returns to Texas a changed man who is not yet eighteen.

The last four words of the book are the last four words of the Nicene Creed, a traditional part of the Catholic mass. McCarthy's decision to make such a strong allusion is fascinating. His works, although heavily influenced by Catholicism, have been critical of its orthodoxy. In this concluding context, the incorporation of the words "the world to come" resonate in such a way that they seem to condemn Cole to the depths of permanent, irrevocable loss.

DISCUSSION QUESTIONS

- How are McCarthy's aesthetics of the West in this novel different from the West in *Blood Meridian*?
- What is the nature of John Grady Cole's romantic character in relation to horses, ranching, and Alejandra?
- What is the nature of the friendship between Lacey Rawlins and John Grady Cole?
- What is compelling about the differences between John Grady Cole's ranch and Don Hector's ranch?
- Why does the aunt intervene in the love affair between John and Alejandra?
- What is the nature of beauty in this novel?
- What happened to John Grady Cole's father and mother?
- What is the significance of John's expertise with horses and chess?

9

THE CROSSING
(1994)

The Crossing is the second volume of McCarthy's self-titled Border Trilogy. Set in 1938, this modern Western covers seven years. The precise passage of time relative to the narrative events is somewhat ambiguous. The narrative is relayed through the omniscient third-person voice that has, by this point in his writing career, become a hallmark of McCarthy's work. This narrator uses language and vocabulary that is more sophisticated than that of the characters, who often use slang and speak in the local dialect. The novel is divided into four sections. Each section follows the action of the protagonist, Billy Parham, as he makes several journeys from his family ranch across the border into Mexico and back again. Page numbers cited for *The Crossing* are from the 1995 paperback edition (New York: First Vintage International).

When the story begins, Parham is fifteen years old and living with his parents and brother, Boyd, on the family cattle ranch in a New Mexico border town. Like John Grady Cole, the Texan protagonist from *All the Pretty Horses*, McCarthy casts Parham as a young romantic who is attached to the grandeur of the American West. Like the evolution of Cole, McCarthy attentively develops a depth to Billy's character by describing his love for ranching and the wilderness. This love for the wilderness is poignantly rendered in the attachment Billy nurtures for a female wolf who has become a nuisance on the ranch.

The wolf has been killing the family's cattle, and Billy's dad has charged him with trapping and killing it. At this point in American history, wolves had been trapped and hunted out of existence in the American West. The only wolves that remained in North America survived in either Canada or Mexico. After Billy traps the she-wolf, he makes a spontaneous decision to return the live animal to Mexico. This decision sparks the series of events that constitute the rest of the narrative.

Over the course of the next seven years, Billy makes three trips out of New Mexico into Mexico. During the first, he tries to repatriate the wolf. During the second, he and his brother Boyd, who is two years younger than Billy, go in search of horses stolen from their father's ranch. The two brothers separate; Billy returns to New Mexico while Boyd remains in Mexico. In his final trip, Billy goes in search of Boyd, who at this point has been living south of the border for several years. As the narrative progresses, McCarthy uses secondary characters to embellish the story with environmental, historical, and theological themes. These themes often are communicated to Billy by people he meets in his travels. These themes imbue the story with an epic dimension that further differentiates it from *All the Pretty Horses*.

In the first of the novel's four sections, Billy traps the wolf and tries to take it back to Mexico, where he thinks it will be free. Billy's love for the she-wolf sharply conflicts with the creed of Western ranchers, who sought to kill every last wolf in America. Though Billy's attempt to return the wolf is driven by noble impulses, those impulses have tragic consequences for him and for all of his family. The book's narrator poignantly foreshadows these consequences at the beginning of the second section with these opening words: "Doomed enterprises forever divide lives between the then and the now" (*The Crossing*, 129).

Cormac McCarthy may have adapted Billy's moral confusion about trapping and disposing of the wolf from a first person narrative by E. T. Seton. In the essay "King of Currumpaw" from his collection *Wild Animals I Have Known*, Seton writes about an outlaw wolf in Northern New Mexico. Seton, an expert wolf trapper, experienced and chronicled tremendous remorse after trapping a wolf he called "Lobo Rex." Seton captured the live wolf by lashing its jaw shut in a manner similar to what Billy does to the she-wolf in *The Crossing*. Lobo Rex was the last wolf Seton ever trapped. After the animal died in captivity, he became a prominent conservationist and eventually founded the Boy Scouts.

Billy's attempt to return the wolf is punctuated by many episodes, but the most significant is when he is stopped by Mexican authorities who confiscate the wolf. Up until this point, Billy's journey has been idyllic. He has languished in the pastoral open plains, sleeping in the night air alongside his horse and the wolf. Billy bound the wolf's mouth for the duration of the trip, but she is not caged. She is tethered to Billy's saddle, and walks timidly behind the horse.

The Mexican authorities take the wolf under the pretense of taking her to a fair. Billy learns that the wolf is being used in a staged dogfight. This knowledge is innocence lost. In what might be one of the saddest episodes in his entire body of work, McCarthy pits the she-wolf, which is noticeably pregnant, against an endless string of vicious dogs for the enjoyment of the crowd. Billy manages to stop the fighting, yet McCarthy's narrative emphasizes this ultimate perversion of the modern human relationship with the natural world. By the end of the book's first section, Billy's quest with the wolf has come to a tragic end.

Near the beginning of the second section, Billy returns home from his several months in Mexico. He finds that while he was gone, his parents were murdered in their house, and their cattle and horses have disappeared. His brother, Boyd, survived. Although the murderers' identities are never revealed, Boyd and Billy believe their parents were killed by men connected to an Indian who came to the Parham ranch begging for food. With their parents dead and the livestock gone, Billy and Boyd are rootless. They leave the ranch in search of the family's horses. Together they cross the border into Mexico.

Eventually, the brothers stumble upon the horses in a Mexican town. The horses allegedly have been bought by a Mexican landowner. Billy and Boyd attempt to free the horses from the Mexican and return with them to New Mexico. Before they can capture the horses, the brothers rescue a Mexican girl from certain rape and murder, an episode which concludes the second section and eventually results in Boyd and Billy drifting away from each other.

The third section begins with Billy and Boyd plotting to release the horses. During this episode, McCarthy departs from the conventions of the Western genre by mixing physical action with philosophical content. This is evident when Boyd is shot as they try to capture their father's animals. The action is supplanted by Billy's prayers for his brother. Billy takes Boyd to a house in a nearby Mexican town to recover from his wound. He then, on Boyd's request, tracks down the girl and brings her back to him. They fall in love, a harbinger of doom for McCarthy's male characters. Several days later, Boyd and the girl abandon Billy. He never sees them alive again. Billy returns to New Mexico.

As the fourth section opens, Billy is alone in New Mexico. It is the early years of American involvement in World War II. Billy and a former neighbor are talking about a mutual acquaintance who enlisted. Billy asks if he's going to be assigned to the cavalry. His neighbor says, "I don't think so. I don't think they're even going to have one" (*The Crossing*, 344). The exchange illustrates Billy's naivete, which persists despite all he has experienced.

Billy then decides to join the U.S. Army. He fails the military physical three times. During the physical, he learns he has a heart murmur that disqualifies him from service. Dejected, he decides to make his third and final trip to Mexico in search of his brother. He returns to some of the places where he and Boyd had traveled together. In one of the towns, he meets a man who tells him of the death of his brother. The man, who is not a Mexican, claims that Boyd was killed in a gunfight several years earlier. The girl escaped.

A Mexican woman tells Billy where to find Boyd's grave. He then digs up what he presumes to be Boyd's bones and brings them back to New Mexico. In the process of repatriating Boyd's remains, Billy is accosted by some bandits, one of whom plunges a knife into the chest of Billy's horse. This gruesome chest wound symbolizes the need for strength in an unjust world. This particular theme reverberates in Boyd's wound and in Billy's heart murmur, both of which hint at injustice.

Embedded in the narrative driving Billy's three trips into Mexico is a meditation by the author on the nature of God and a higher order to human existence. Each of Billy's three separate journeys is punctuated by a seemingly random convergence of events. In the first trip, he discovers the dog-fighting arena and his wolf. In the second, he and Boyd stumble upon their father's horses. In the third, he finds a grave that contains what he believes to be his brother's bones. It is precisely through this randomness that McCarthy suggests the existence of a deep structure providing order to human lives.

In addition to random events, McCarthy's secondary characters communicate this philosophy of a higher order. When Billy is returning from his first trip into Mexico, he meets a man who lives in a ruined church. The man functions as a prophetic character who shares his wisdom about the natural order of the world. He tells Billy that people have not sufficiently inquired into "miracles of destruction." An important theological aspect of the novel develops from this quote, which is that religious people misunderstand the actions of God. The man vigorously asserts that God is more violent and vengeful than people want to believe. This view of God is an important theme in the novel.

Ultimately, Billy's journey, in which fate or God has a heavy hand, is a sad and painful coming of age story—the *bildungsroman*. At the end

Cormac McCarthy updates his sense of the American pastoral to incorporate the environmental history of the wolf in America. At the point when the novel begins, 1938, all known wolves had been trapped and killed in the lower 48 states. McCarthy and Edward Abbey reportedly tried to reintroduce wolves, illegally, in New Mexico. American author Barry Lopez verified this rumor in a personal conversation (February 25, 2008). Another source for McCarthy's depiction of wolves and wolf behavior is Lopez's classic study, *Of Wolves and Men*.

of the story, Billy's naivete and loneliness emphasize his anachronistic nature. To survive, he has to grow up. But even when Billy decides he wants to stop being a cowboy and become a soldier, he cannot because of his birth defect. The crushing irony of his predicament is brought home for the reader during an episode toward the end of the novel. Billy, about to return to Mexico for the final time, is drinking in a bar when another patron accuses him of dodging the draft. Billy bears the insults with a silent stoicism, choosing not to defend himself verbally or physically. Despite his heroics—defending his father's honor, returning to Mexico to find his brother—he is denied admission into the cult of manhood that is defined by military service.

This alienation from the male world is compounded by Billy's alienation from the animal world, which may have been one of the only sources of comfort for him in the novel. Billy's connection to the animal world is poignantly represented by the heroic and loving efforts of the family dog, who follows Billy for two-thirds of the novel and then disappears. The closing scene of the novel, which takes place in a barn in the year 1945, may provide a clue into the meaning inherent in the animal's absence.

Billy's aimless wandering has led him to bed down in an abandoned barn inhabited by an ancient and decrepit dog, which McCarthy describes as the "repository of a thousand indignities." Billy chases the dog out of the barn and then, realizing his inhuman transgression, runs out into the night calling for it, but it is gone. It is unclear whether or not this is indeed the Parhams' dog. There are some reasons to support both points of view. What is most important is Billy's reaction, because his rejection of the dog is a momentary instance when he loses his romantic heart and ultimately forsakes what might be the only living remnant of his family besides his horse. Billy's regret is palpable and is the final stage of his tragic loss of innocence. His cruelty to the dog hints at the debased human world that McCarthy portrays in the final novel of the trilogy, *Cities of the Plain*.

DISCUSSION QUESTIONS

- How does the pastoralism of McCarthy's Southern gothic novels differ from the ecological representation of the she-wolf?
- Why does Billy decide to take the wolf back to Mexico?
- Discuss the nature of Billy's trips into Mexico.
- What is the irony of Billy being denied service in the military?
- Why do Billy and Boyd try to recapture the family horses?
- Why does Boyd leave Billy?
- Why does Billy kill the wolf?
- Why does Billy chase the dog away at the end of the novel?
- How does McCarthy develop or alter the stereotype of the cowboy in this novel?

10

CITIES OF THE PLAIN
(1998)

Cities of the Plain, the final novel of the Border Trilogy, brings together the protagonists of the first two novels, John Grady Cole and Billy Parham. Page numbers cited for *Cities of the Plain* are from the 1998 hardcover edition (New York: Alfred A. Knopf).

Chronologically, the story opens roughly four years after the end of *All the Pretty Horses.* In *Cities of the Plain,* Parham and Cole are working together on the Cross Fours ranch, which is run and owned by Mac McGovern, a kind man who values the skills of Parham and especially Cole. At this point Cole is twenty and Parham is twenty-eight. The central conflict of the novel is Cole's love affair with an epileptic Mexican prostitute, Magdalena. The love affair is, like all of McCarthy's fictional relationships between men and women, doomed. Parham tries to save Cole from tragedy, but he is unable to dissuade his friend from pursuing Magdalena. After Cole's death, the novel jumps ahead several decades to the year 2002, where an aged Billy Parham is starring as an extra in a movie.

Cities of the Plain never received the critical acclaim that the first two installments of the Border Trilogy did. Arguably, *All the Pretty Horses,* with its lyricism and romance, and *The Crossing,* with its adventurous and philosophic nature, set the critical bar rather high for the author. The book faced an additional challenge in that, unlike its predecessors, *Cities of the Plain* is not wholly original. This last story in the

> The final installment of the Border Trilogy, *Cities of the Plain* began as a screenplay.

trilogy evolves from the narratives that constituted the first two stories. In fact, many narrative episodes and characters that appear in *Cities of the Plain* can be found in the previous two novels. This repetition renders the archetypes, stereotypes, and narrative events in a slightly diminished form.

In the first two novels, John Grady Cole and Billy Parham exist as mystical and romantic adventurers. Both characters experience a coming of age in the original works. In *Cities of the Plain*, the adult men are working side by side on a cattle ranch in southern New Mexico along the Mexican border. The story begins in 1952. They live a meager, hard-scrabble existence on the ranch, and their lives as ranch hands are set in stark contrast against modernity. Their livelihood is being threatened with extinction. The U.S. government has laid claims to McGovern's ranch with plans to take it over for the military. This looming eventuality undermines the sense of domestic stability that Cole and Parham have found on the ranch.

Instead of the high romance of the previous two novels, a serious melancholy hovers over the entirety of this narrative. The two men who have been thwarted in their ambitions stubbornly resist the reality of their failures in the modern age. The novel develops the friendship between Billy and John. They engage in brotherly and friendly banter around the ranch. Yet, Cole and Parham tell each other little about their past adventures. McCarthy uses the technique of dramatic irony, in which the audience is aware of facts that the characters are not.

Cole seems much like the same character readers knew at the end of *All the Pretty Horses*, but it is Parham who has changed the most from his rendering at the end of *The Crossing*. Parham has transformed from a stoic outsider to a regular cowboy. He is now self-conscious and ironic and says things like: "I love this life," "You do love this life don't you? Cause by God I love it." The comic and world-weary tone Parham affects differs starkly from his character's sparse, detached dialogue in *The Crossing*.

Even though both characters are still young men, they seem much older than they are. The powerful innocence and iconoclasm that defined both young men are gone, replaced by an unsettling strain of social conformity. For example, the novel opens with the two of them sitting in a bar with their friend Troy, picking out fat whores. Gone is the high romance of Cole's relationship with Alejandra and Boyd's (Parham's brother) relationship with the Mexican girl. In its place is a debased and cruel mockery of the male and female companionship.

After this episode in the bar, McCarthy continues to repeat previous episodes from the first two books of the Border Trilogy with slight alterations. For example, instead of wild wolves threatening livestock, which drove the narrative in *The Crossing*, feral dogs are killing McGovern's cattle. In an episode that mirrors one from *All the Pretty Horses*, Cole again finds himself struggling for his life in an epic knife fight in Mexico. In another episode that mirrors one from *All the Pretty Horses*, John Grady Cole engages in intensive games of chess with McGovern. McCarthy's re-use of chess underscores that Cole's character is a cowboy with a powerful intellect; however, much less is at stake in these games than when Cole played against Alejandra's Aunt. McGovern cannot offer Cole a place in a family or society that Cole fervently desires. The games merely solidify Cole's status as an anachronism—as a cowboy on a doomed ranch. McCarthy does not attach such symbolism to the character of Billy Parham in *Cities of the Plain* until the end of the novel.

In another episode that pulls together narrative devices from the first two books in the series, Cole falls in love with a woman outside of his social class—a Mexican prostitute named Magdalena, and Parham tries to rescue him from this doomed relationship, just as he tried to save his brother Boyd from the doomed relationship with the *bandida*.

Cole does not mean to fall in love with Magdalena, but he does. He visits Magdalena several times, and Cole learns that her life is controlled by a menacing pimp, named Eduardo. The tension between Cole and Eduardo is heightened when Cole learns that Eduardo is also in love with Magdalena. When Cole tells Parham that he has fallen in love, Parham becomes furious with Cole. He blames himself, because he took Cole to the Mexican brothel where Magdalena works. Parham also is despairing because he and Cole both know that if Eduardo learns of Cole's feelings, he will kill him.

Despite the danger, Cole persists in pursuing a life with Magdalena. He asks McGovern whether he can have a ruined little adobe hut on the ranch. Parham helps him restore the hut. After the place has been refurbished, Parham tries to help Cole purchase Magdalena's freedom from Eduardo. Cole returns to Mexico to bring Magdalena home, only to find

Cities of the Plain is an allusion to Genesis 19:29, where God destroys the cities of Sodom and Gomorrah.

that Eduardo has discovered their plan and killed her as she tried to escape.

In the culminating action—which is the most dramatic in the novel—Cole dies in a knife fight with Eduardo. His death is not immediate. Parham finds him as he is slowly bleeding to death. Tragically innocent to the very end, Cole sought to save Magdalena from her wretched existence. His pastoral vision dies unrealized with him.

The novel then jumps ahead about fifty years to realize its rather bleak end. Parham, now an old man, has found work as an extra in a movie. He is homeless and lives alone. The book concludes with a scene where a family takes him in. This ending is an apt elegy for Billy Parham. At the end of the book, he says to the woman who is caring for him, "I'm not what you think I am. I aint nothing. I dont know why you put up with me." She responds, "Well, Mr Parham. I know who you are. And I do know why. You go to sleep now" (*Cities of the Plain*, 292). He is the embodiment of the final remnant of the romantic origins of the culture of the American West. And that culture has all but disappeared.

Billy's difficult survival into old age represents an important theme in the next novel by McCarthy. In *No Country for Old Men*, McCarthy ruminates on the psychological effects of age being a factor in making one feel out of place in a particular time.

DISCUSSION QUESTIONS

- What events in *Cities of the Plain* does McCarthy reprise from the preceding novels of the Border Trilogy?
- Why does McCarthy employ so much narrative repetition?
- What connection is there between McCarthy beginning this novel as a screenplay and Billy Parham being an extra in a movie?
- What does the end of Billy's life tell us about the modern cowboy?
- What's the significance of the knife fight with Eduardo?
- How do we see the idea of the pastoral developed in the representation of Mac's ranch and in Cole's refurbishing of a little house for him and Magdalena?
- What is the significance of the biblical allusion in the title of this book?
- How do the romantic quests in this novel differ from *All the Pretty Horses* and *The Crossing*?

11

NO COUNTRY FOR OLD MEN
(2005)

With the publication of *No Country for Old Men*, McCarthy solidified his transition from critically acclaimed, best-selling author to popular national writer. Through his imaginative forays into commercial genres, like the Western in the Border Trilogy, McCarthy has garnered popular success in this later stage of his career. Instead of the Western, in this book McCarthy employs elements of detective fiction—an unsolved crime, moral ambiguity, violence, and an action-driven narrative. The book is written for a general audience, without the use of heavy language or complicated allegory that was prominent in his earlier works (for example, *Outer Dark* and *Blood Meridian*). However, that does not mean the book lacks philosophical content. In *No Country for Old Men*, McCarthy creates a morality play that uses the seductiveness and corruption of the drug trade as narrative devices. Page numbers cited for *No Country for Old Men* are from the 2005 hardcover edition (New York: Alfred A. Knopf).

Anton Chigurh, a psychopathic killer, is the criminal mastermind, and Bell, a west Texas sheriff, is the ethical lawman. The story pits Bell's traditional law-abiding values against what appears to be Chigurh's nihilistic and savage ideology. Caught in the crossfire between these two men is Llewellyn Moss, a military veteran and romantic outsider, who has

> The novel takes its title from the first line of W. B. Yeats's poem "Sailing to Byzantium," which is, "That is no country for old men." The poem is Yeats's meditation on the relationship between aging, death, the soul, and the importance of art as a way of redeeming mortality. Yeats's love for the ancient and beautiful city of Byzantium contrasts with the artlessness and ugliness of the drug war on the border of Texas and Mexico. Yet, Sheriff Bell's character is heroic, like the speaker in Yeats's poem, in how he faces old age.

stumbled upon $2 million in drug money in the Texas desert. Chigurh and Bell are both hunting Moss; Chigurh to kill him, Moss to save him.

Sheriff EdTom Bell, a lifelong lawman, is overwhelmed, emotionally and tactically, by the escalating violence of the drug trade along the U.S.-Mexican border. The action begins sometime in the early 1980s when Llewellyn Moss discovers the carnage of a botched drug deal, including a case filled with money, while hunting antelope in the desert. Moss, a Vietnam Veteran in his thirties, who lives in the same town as Bell, knows that if he takes the money, he and his young wife, Carla Jean, will be hunted to the death. Chigurh, a bounty hunter and professional assassin, is hired to track and kill him. Chigurh is a mysterious, unsettling character with an almost mystical efficiency at dispatching his victims. His employer is unknown. His weapon of choice is a tool used in slaughterhouses to fell cattle, which, by its design, ensures that Chigurh must be in close physical contact with his victims.

McCarthy structures the story using dual narratives that follow Moss on the run and Bell on his trail. McCarthy employs the same physical setting of his previous four books, the American Southwest, but he populates this setting with a modern cast of characters. During certain episodes, the characters cross the border between the United States and Mexico, but in this modern era, border crossings involve gates, fences, and the Border Patrol; seamless passage belongs to a bygone era. The novel exhibits a prose that is sparser than any of his prior novels and features the absence of quotation marks and most apostrophes that have become his signature technique. Late in his career, he is still experimenting with style—for the first time, he employs extended interior monologues to develop his protagonist, Sheriff Bell.

In addition to this new narrative technique, McCarthy also is exploring new philosophical territory. Unlike the *bildungsroman*, which dominated most of his Western and Southern gothic works, the characters in

No Country are adults. As such, they are held accountable for their actions within a society that metes out justice based on an unwavering definition of right and wrong. The narrative is uncomplicated; the characters are realistic.

The story is a morality play, with a twist: Bell is the embodiment of good, but he is tired and unprepared for the challenges of modern society. At first blush, Chigurh's behavior appears to be purely evil, but McCarthy challenges this assumption by stripping Chigurh of all motivations. Chigurh claims that fate has placed his victims in his path. By killing his victims, he is neither good nor bad, right nor wrong; he is beyond reproach.

However, the philosophy Chigurh espouses does not fit seamlessly with his actions. Chigurh is a horror undeserving of reader sympathy. In one of the book's opening episodes, McCarthy renders Chigurh's murderous nature in gruesome detail. Chigurh allows himself to be captured by a deputy merely to see if he can escape. He does so by strangling the deputy to death while still in a pair of handcuffs. This is as vicious and disconcerting of a beginning as McCarthy has written and seems to leave no ambiguity about Chigurh's moral nature.

The action and realism of the narrative are repeatedly suspended by Sheriff Bell's musings during a series of philosophical digressions. Stylistically, these digressions are set apart from the main narrative in italics. By allowing Bell these introspective moments, McCarthy imbues him with a higher moral authority than the other characters in the book. Bell reflects on the changing nature of society, how he is shocked by the behavior of ordinary citizens, and how the world as he thought he knew it has all but disappeared. In contrast, Chigurh, before he kills his victims, engages them in philosophical games of cat and mouse as part of the action. He chastises his victims for their moral failings while insisting that their fate was predetermined, which is why he must kill them. Bell's musings bear witness to a world that is going from good to bad; Chigurh's very presence affirms those thoughts. But, according to Chigurh, both men are merely playing the role fate has assigned to them.

Llewellyn Moss exhibits several characteristics typical of McCarthy's male protagonists. He is stoic, resourceful, and pragmatic. He has exceptional survival skills. For example, Moss is more than just a good shot with a rifle; he was a sniper in Vietnam. Moss loots the scene of a drug deal during which all but one of the members of both parties kill each other. He finds the one man who is still alive in a truck but does not help him. After surveying the scene, Moss figures that only a lot of money could be the cause of so much carnage, and he proceeds to find it. Moss takes the money back to his trailer, where his wife, Carla Jean, is waiting for him.

> McCarthy wrote this novel while he was a fellow at the Santa Fe Institute.

In the middle of the night, Moss decides to return to the scene of the gunfight. Why he goes is a little murky, despite a few omniscient passages, and his return remains an ethical mystery that drives the rest of the story. The reader is left to wonder whether Moss went back to help the lone survivor or to kill him to make sure his tracks are covered. Resolution of this moral quandary is the reader's responsibility. Moss tries to return stealthily, but the site of the botched deal has been staked out by associates of the drug dealers. They spot Moss, and the chase begins. It is an asymmetric game of hunter and hunted between, Moss, the Mexicans, Chigurh, and Bell.

Chigurh pursues Moss, and as he does so, the bodies pile up. In an effort to get to Moss, he also hunts down Carla Jean. Contrasted with Chigurh's unswervingly murderous arc is Sheriff Bell, the only character who seems morally incorruptible, but he is overwhelmed by the ongoing slaughter. Bell is a veteran of World War II. As a member of the Greatest Generation, he stands as an astonished witness to the carnage that the drug trade has created in his county. For example, as he and his deputy are surveying the botched drug deal that Moss first found, his deputy says "It's a mess, ain't it Sherriff?" To which Sheriff Bell responds, "If it ain't it'll do until a mess gets here" (*No Country for Old Men*, 77).

McCarthy moves outside the tradition of the detective genre in his construct of the main narrative and in the story's resolution. Both are unconventional. Throughout the book, the main characters rarely interact with each other, and there is no confrontation or showdown between any of the main characters. The story ends with Bell's final musing, and Chigurh disappears to continue to mete out his version of justice on the deserving. The outcome of the struggle between good and evil in the Texas desert remains unresolved. This cosmic moral struggle becomes even more pronounced in McCarthy's next novel, a dark story of survival in a postapocalyptic world.

DISCUSSION QUESTIONS

- Why does Moss return the money?
- What are Chigurh's principles?

- How do Bell's monologues develop his character?
- Why does McCarthy leave the struggle between Bell and Chigurh unresolved?
- What is the significance of Chigurh killing people with a bolt gun used for slaughtering cattle?
- What parts of the narrative are unresolved?
- What genres does McCarthy combine in this novel?

12

THE ROAD
(2007)

Cormac McCarthy's tenth novel, *The Road*, solidified his legacy as a major American author. This book, published when McCarthy was seventy-four, won the 2007 Pulitzer Prize for fiction. Late in his career, McCarthy earned one of the most coveted international accolades awarded to works of fiction. Page numbers cited for *The Road* are from the 2006 hardcover edition (New York: Alfred A. Knopf).

In this work, McCarthy demonstrates how precisely he has honed his stylistic trademarks of a simple narrative and sparse prose. The setting is bleak and postapocalyptic. The story features strong biblical overtones within the context of what many critics have claimed to be McCarthy's most compelling and complex relationship between two fictional characters, a middle-age father and his young son.

The Road's central conflict is that an unnamed disaster—in all probability a nuclear holocaust—has created a nuclear winter on earth. The story is set in America where all traces of modern society have stopped functioning. There is no electricity; there is no gasoline; there are no factories or stores or automobiles. Anarchy reigns in this desolate ash-covered world where the sun has been blotted from the sky.

The main characters are nameless. The boy calls his father "Papa." In his thoughts, the father refers to his son as "the boy." Together, the two slowly plod south in search of warmer weather on the southern

One notable place that the boy and his father pass through is Rock City, Tennessee. Tennessee was Cormac McCarthy's home state for several decades.

coast because the father is convinced that they will not survive the encroaching winter. They push their meager belongings, which includes a well-worn and oft-consulted map, in a creaky shopping cart down the middle of barren roads coated with debris. The ensuing cold and lack of sunlight has killed everything except a small number of people. To survive, some people have resorted to cannibalism. Thus, a new social order has evolved, one segmented into the "good guys," who try to survive by scavenging, and the "bad guys," who kill humans for meat.

This new social order creates for a harrowing journey through the wastes of America. The father knows the risks they will face by pursuing this journey, but he feels they have no choice. Armed with a pistol and two bullets, the father is determined to protect his son from the gruesome realities of this brave new world. They face many obstacles together, and their search for hope in a world where there is none to be had is both heart rending and inspiring.

The story is told through a combination of omniscient third-person narration and the father's first-person perspective. McCarthy also uses flashback scenes to fill in some of the story's detail in the form of the father's dream sequences. From one of these sequences, readers learn that the son was born shortly after the global catastrophe occurred. Several years after her son's birth, the mother committed suicide. Her decision to end her life was driven by the psychological and physical exhaustion of struggling to survive in the postapocalyptic reality.

The story suggests that the mother's decision to kill herself was one made in the name of love, not cowardice. She died to improve her son's and husband's odds of survival. She is physically and emotionally distraught when her husband is preparing for their departure and knows her weakness will make the trio vulnerable to attack from the bad guys. She also knows that after eight years of survivalist living, her husband has only two bullets left in his .22. The family lives in constant fear of being captured, raped, killed, and eaten. The two remaining bullets are a last resort. The father can use them to kill the boy and then himself.

Within this context of total social and environmental collapse, McCarthy explores the nature and origin of the human impulse to survive in the face of hopelessness. The father's thoughts convey a torturous and desperate internal monologue with and about God. The man alternates between offering up prayers to and hurling curses at the Almighty. Between and during these internal rants, the man's love for his child is an unwaveringly powerful and bittersweet life force. Ultimately, the man believes that the very existence of his child is proof of a living God, and he will endure untold suffering and sacrifice to spare his child the horrors of the world they inhabit.

The power of *The Road* resides in the precise clarity with which McCarthy has rendered the destruction of the known world. Simple episodes overwhelm with powerful nostalgia. For example, early in the story, the father finds one last can of Coca-Cola in a vending machine that has been plundered by survivors. The boy has never had a Coke before. He sits his son down. And he offers him the drink. The boy exclaims: "It's bubbly" (*The Road*, 20). At his son's urging, the father takes a sip from the can and hands it back. Then the two sit together while the son finishes the soda. The boy says to his father that he knows he'll never have another Coca-Cola. The father does not answer directly. The gentle beauty of this simple windfall evaporates and is replaced by dread. The episode is magnificently rendered.

During their travels, father and son discover a house in which cannibals are storing, dismembering, and gradually eating people. The scene is a horror show and emphasizes the futility of the father's quest to behave nobly in a debased world. He is surrounded by evil. Soon after this episode, and only a few days from starvation, the man and son discover an underground bunker. It is a pristine gold mine, untouched by the hordes of scavengers that preceded them. The bunker has a hatch that can be sealed from the inside. It is stocked with clothes, food, whiskey, coffee, and bullets—but none for a .22. There is no gun. The father knows there is no gun to be found. Without the gun, there is no safety for father and son.

McCarthy renders the windfall of the bunker in striking contrast to the cannibals' basement. The discovery of the bunker is one of the more powerful episodes in the narrative because the boy and his father are almost at their psychological and physical limits. In the episodes leading

McCarthy tells Oprah the story of the composition of the novel. He was in a hotel room in El Paso, when he awoke around 4:00 a.m. and saw lights on the horizon. He imagined that there had been a nuclear holocaust. This image stuck in his mind. About a year later, he started writing this book when he was in Ireland. He said he wrote it in about three months. When he started writing, he said that he realized that he had been writing it in his head for more than a year.

McCarthy dedicated this book to his son John, which marks the first time he has dedicated a book to any person.

up to the discovery of the underground bunker, McCarthy explores in painful detail the human capacity for suffering. He pushes his characters up to the end—to the brink of starvation and despair—gives them a brief respite from the deprivation, and then pushes them back out into the harsh cold world. They must continue their quest for survival against insurmountable odds.

The Road concludes in dramatic fashion with the death of the father and the torturous and improbable survival of the son, who is discovered by a man who has a family. The man, as we see him, is one of the great and enduring images of the novel, if not in all of McCarthy's novels. As he approaches the boy, his shotgun is visible, as is a bandolier of shells, which have been repacked and sealed with candle wax. The left side of his face bears a huge scar, evidence of a possible skirmish with pipe-wielding cannibals. He is one of the good guys, a powerful final statement about the persistence of good in a world filled with evil. The boy survives, and with him, hope persists.

These elemental themes—good versus evil, the persistence of hope—are essential components of this and other works by McCarthy. He infuses classical themes with a modern vitality. Yet, this novel takes it one step further. The book ends with a short metaphor that addresses humanity's relationship with the natural world.

The final paragraph of the book is supplied by an omniscient narrator. The narrator describes a vanished natural world using brook trout as a metaphor. The narrator describes the brook trout as an ancient creature on whose flesh was etched the map of the world "in its becoming" (*The Road*, 241). The brook trout, and the mystery of life and evolution which they embodied, have been destroyed by humans. And that destruction can never be undone.

This concluding passage evokes the yearning for the pastoral with which McCarthy has imbued all of his published work. The image of the brook trout, which is wholly unconnected to the narrative, is an elegy to a beauty in wilderness that will never exist again, and in this way, the novel's power resonates because it extends beyond the realm of the egocentric concerns of the life and death of human beings into a more universal and cosmic realm. The standard theme of the apocalyptic genre, in which the natural world continues to work and return to "normal" in the absence of human interference, has been turned upside down. At the end of *The Road*, the natural world "could not be made right again."

DISCUSSION QUESTIONS

- What genres does McCarthy combine in *The Road*?
- Why does the man's wife kill herself?
- Given the clues in the story, what do you think caused the environmental collapse?
- Why does McCarthy not name the mother, father, and son?
- What does this story add to McCarthy's statements about the nature of God?
- What does this story add to McCarthy's ideas about people?
- What is the significance of the can of Coca-Cola?

13

DRAMATIC WORKS BY
CORMAC McCARTHY

Cormac McCarthy writes primarily in the fiction genre. He has, however, made several forays into drama. His known dramatic works include one unpublished screenplay, *Whales and Men*; two stage plays, *The Stonemason* and *The Sunset Limited*; and one teleplay, *The Gardener's Son*, which aired on PBS in 1976 and was nominated for two Emmys.

The three published plays lack the virtuosic prose of his novels, yet they develop several themes that are central to McCarthy's authorial vision, such as the challenge of finding meaning in human existence, the problems posed by modernity, and the pastoral element inherent to Southern culture. Women and African Americans play much more prominent roles in McCarthy's dramatic works than they do in his novels, which are exclusively dominated by the romantic quests of males.

WHALES AND MEN (UNPUBLISHED)

As for *Whales and Men*, the only known copy of this unpublished screenplay is housed with McCarthy's papers at Southwest Texas State University. To read the screenplay, written permission from the author is required. Little is known about the screenplay, but what is known has been gleaned from an article by Edwin T. Arnold.

Whales and Men is relatively unknown—written permission from the author is needed to read it. Thus, what McCarthy readers know of this story is based mainly on Edwin T. Arnold's article, "Cormac McCarthy's *Whales and Men*." The play has two possible sources, Lopez's essay, "A Presentation of Whales" from his collection *Crossing Open Ground*, and Roger Payne's book *Among Whales*. McCarthy also knows Roger Payne—both were recipients of MacArthur awards. *Whales and Men* echoes the title of Barry Lopez's book *Of Wolves and Men*.

The story is a modernized version of a novel McCarthy has cited as one of his greatest influences, Melville's *Moby Dick*. Written sometime in the mid-1980s, it involves a cast of male and female characters aboard a research vessel who are studying whales for their philosophical and scientific value. The plot features Guy Shuler, a marine biologist, and his friends John Western and Peter Gregory. John Western's girlfriend, Kelly McAmon, also has a prominent role in the story.

The story is set aboard the vessel in Florida, Ireland, and Colombo, Sri Lanka. The plot's main action centers on this group's interest in a pod of blue whales in particular, which the vessel tracks across an oceanic journey. This pod is attacked by a whaling ship, and the mother of a young blue whale is killed. The carnage horrifies the research group, who witness the attack. The dramatic tension heightens when the now-motherless baby whale is threatened by an impending shark attack. The screenplay explores the effects this violence has on the emotional and philosophical development of the different characters.

Despite the flawed nature of the screenplay—Arnold claims that its long philosophical passages would make filming difficult—it foreshadows the concerns with environmental degradation caused by human negligence and abuse that McCarthy explores in *The Crossing* and *The Road*.

THE GARDENER'S SON (WRITTEN 1975–76, TELEVISED 1976, PUBLISHED 1996)

McCarthy wrote *The Gardener's Son* at the request of Richard Pearce, the film's director. Pearce, a documentary filmmaker, was familiar with McCarthy's early novels. He was particularly taken with *Child of God*. Based on those works, he wrote to McCarthy in 1975 and invited him to participate in what would be the director's first foray into a fiction film. McCarthy agreed. The two men traveled through South Carolina together, visiting textile mills and the small towns that housed them, researching what would ultimately become the teleplay. The two-hour film took a year to write and shoot and was nominated for two Emmy Awards.

In his introduction to the published teleplay, Pearce writes that the story was based on "a few paragraphs in the footnotes to a 1928 biography of a famous industrialist of the pre–Civil War South." With a cast of more than forty characters, McCarthy tries to create the realistic social fabric of a small mill town in Graniteville, South Carolina. The conflict centers around the utopian experiment of the Greggs—the family that founded the cotton mill—who sought to create a work environment that was mutually beneficial for both owner and worker. Over the course of two generations, violence and the Great Depression gradually destroy this utopian experiment.

The main character, Robert McEvoy is a bitter man, who has lost a limb working in the mill. He blames the son of the mill owner for this accident. McEvoy leaves town, and when he returns, he finds his father working on the assembly line and not as the mill's gardener, which was his previous position. Crippled and angry, McEvoy stokes a burning rage for the Gregg family, which drives the action.

The Gardener's Son pits antebellum agrarian values in the character of McEvoy against the Greggs' Protestant work ethic and Yankee industrialism. Through the play's conclusion, both value systems are undermined when McEvoy kills the mill owner. Through McEvoy, McCarthy again explores the inevitability of man's violence against man within the context of a social structure that is slowly dissolving.

THE STONEMASON (1994)

Almost twenty years after *The Gardener's Son*, McCarthy published his next play—this time for the stage. With *The Stonemason*, published in 1994, McCarthy again demonstrates his personal interest in the way in which individuals have become disconnected from their labor and work in modern society. He explores this theme repeatedly in his novels, especially in connection with ideas about Southern pastoralism.

In *The Stonemason*, McCarthy explores this theme of modernity as a cause of social disconnect from the perspective of a black family, the Telfairs. The play is set in Louisville, Kentucky, in the 1970s. The Telfairs are stonemasons, a trade that, because of the arcane and highly specialized knowledge it requires, is increasingly anachronistic in the modern

Reportedly, McCarthy lived with a family of black stonemasons to learn the craft. Presumably, he learned enough to build a hearth and chimney from the stones that he scavenged from James Agee's condemned house in Knoxville, Tennessee.

world. The play's story features the conflict between four generations of Telfair men and their families, all of whom live under one roof, as they struggle to adapt to a changing society in which their ancestral trade is of little value.

The story is told from the perspective of Ben, age thirty-two, who abandoned his education and his goal of becoming a school teacher to return to Louisville and learn the family trade. Papaw is the oldest of the Telfair men and, like his father before him, has worked as a stonemason his whole life. Papaw's son and Ben's father, Big Ben, is a contractor and uses Ben's and Papaw's labor to run his business. A fifteen-year-old nephew, Soldier, is further removed from the family profession by drug addiction. The play relays the financial and emotional turmoil the family experiences as their social fabric slowly unravels.

The Stonemason has never been staged. Set to open in the early 1990s, production stopped for a variety of reasons. In his essay "Cormac McCarthy's *The Stonemason*: The Unmaking of a Play," in *A Cormac McCarthy Companion*, Edwin T. Arnold chronicles the aesthetic and ideological conflicts involved with rehearsing, interpreting, and staging the play. Two black female actors objected to the representation of black women in the play and as a result dropped out of the performance. In addition, the director and other actors asked McCarthy to rewrite parts of the play, in part because the numerous stages it required were too complex. McCarthy agreed to do so, but he worked slowly and was loath to rewrite as much as he was asked. In a final and surprising move, the theater troupe returned a $25,000 grant that it received to produce the play.

THE SUNSET LIMITED (2006)

McCarthy's second stage play, *The Sunset Limited,* was produced successfully. Published in 2006, *The Sunset Limited* is a dramatic dialogue between two men, who are only known as Black and White. The whole play takes place in Black's New York City apartment. Just a few moments before the opening scene, Black has stopped White from throwing himself in front of a train. Before the suicide attempt, the two men were unknown to each other. The entire play consists of Black trying to talk White out of committing suicide.

The play pits the tough-minded spiritualism of a former criminal and drug addict with a violent history—Black—who has embraced the Bible and chosen to live in the ghetto, against a professor—White—who is overwhelmed by the world, which he sees as godless and devoid of meaning.

The play, which shows McCarthy's ear for dialect and dialogue, is a sympathetic portrayal of both men's lives. The dialogue draws the audience into their respective plights, which shows the black man as the caretaker of humanity and the white man as irredeemably pessimistic. The urban location—a small apartment in a tenement—is an entirely new and constrained setting for the author with none of the rural reference points that defined the scope of all his previous works. The pared-down setting and emotionally laden dialogue are both new techniques for the author, and he employs them to full effect. In May and June of 2006, the renowned Steppenwolf Theatre Company, a well known troupe based in Chicago, staged the play for a five-week run.

Of the many poignant exchanges in the play, one of the most memorable is when Black feeds White some soul food. This is the point at which White is the most human. He enjoys the meal, and the two men talk about something other than suicide. This moment, while not momentous, shows White begrudgingly acknowledging Black's kindness in an inherently inhospitable world. Black shows White unconditional friendship, and White, tragically, rejects it in all of its forms except for the meal.

Although these four important but minor works are of interest primarily to McCarthy devotees, it is quite possible that *The Stonemason* and *The Sunset Limited* eventually will reach national audiences.

DISCUSSION QUESTIONS

- How do McCarthy's dramatic works differ from his fictional works?
- What are McCarthy's environmental concerns?
- What do you think of the conflict regarding the staging of *The Stonemason*?
- How do McCarthy's philosophical tendencies hinder or complement his dramatic works?

14

TODAY'S ISSUES IN CORMAC McCARTHY'S WORK

Contemporary French philosopher and cultural theorist Jean-François Lyotard claims that the fragmented nature of postmodern culture obscures the elemental problem of human survival. And human survival is the elemental issue with which all of Cormac McCarthy's works are concerned. Beginning with his Southern gothic novels up through *The Road*, McCarthy's published books and plays explore both the process through which lone male protagonists survive and the universal forces which affect that survival.

FAMILY AND SOCIETY

Almost all of McCarthy's protagonists have been stripped of or have intentionally relinquished their connections to family and personal history. All exist on the far-flung fringes of organized society and are without any functioning family structure. By placing his characters beyond the reach of civilization, McCarthy has created a space wherein his protagonists, undistracted by the trappings of modern existence, engage in life or death struggles while confronting elemental issues that have challenged human beings since the beginning of recorded history—issues such as human nature and the nature of knowledge, the persistence of good and evil, the existence of God and God's nature, the role of destiny in determining a man's state of being, and the supreme role of violence in realizing that destiny. In his last two novels, McCarthy links these classical themes to two current issues: the drug war and environmental collapse.

The only published works in which McCarthy's characters maintain a connection to family, and thus, society, are *The Stonemason*, *No Country for Old Men*, and *The Road*. In these works, society is collapsing around male protagonists who struggle to survive as embodiments of the force of good against overwhelming odds. Thus, McCarthy has inverted the main issue he addressed in the other works: Instead of a lone outsider struggling to survive, it is the survival of society itself that is at risk for Ben Telfair, Sheriff Bell, and the unnamed father in *The Road*. These three works, therefore, address issues that have caused the fraying of the social fabric. In *The Stonemason*, it is the loss of tradition to encroaching modernity; in *No Country for Old Men*, the drug trade is ripping society apart. But for the father in *The Road*, society has been irrevocably destroyed. The hellish journey he makes alongside his young son prophesies a nightmarish future for humanity in a world in which society has ceased to exist, where evil reigns. This power of evil over good, because of weak social bonds, is one of the defining issues in McCarthy's early work.

McCarthy was writing his Southern gothic works during the 1960s and 1970s, an era of tremendous social and political upheaval in America. At the time, he was living in relative isolation in his native Tennessee and was notoriously disengaged with American society. The books he wrote during this time do not reflect the era's overarching social concerns with the state of race and class and gender in America. Instead, they are concerned with more classical and universal themes such as violence, good and evil, the nature of God, survival, destiny versus human will, self-reliance, and the desire for a pastoral existence.

For most of his career, McCarthy's themes are transcendent and thus do not reflect contemporary issues. Yet, the themes that he represents in his novels show a deep consideration for the ramifications of a weak or nonexistent society. For example, in *The Orchard Keeper*, the dream of a pastoral existence away from the impurities of organized society is continually unreachable for John Wesley Rattner. The best John can do is to survive, which is a pale imitation of the American ideal of self-reliance.

In *Outer Dark*, McCarthy reduces human existence to its most basic levels to show the struggle between good and evil. Again, by stripping away the protection offered by a structured society, he exposes his two protagonists to evil. McCarthy's bleak view in this work shows evil triumphing over good. It is an unsettling perspective because literature, despite the vast range of views embodied in the medium, tends to be life-affirming. McCarthy's antithetical view of humanity contrasts with the general ideas that our culture holds about human nature. Notably, McCarthy composed this novel at the height of the Vietnam War. In this way, the pessimism and despair found in the novel does reflect sentiments shared by some members of American society. While the 1960s counterculture extended into the 1970s, McCarthy's work ignored the trappings of this social and cultural unrest and continued to plumb the depths of the nature of God.

Child of God challenges the extremes of Christian theology and posits the notion of a less-than-benevolent God. McCarthy creates a character in Lester Ballard that is repugnant, yet the book forces readers to consider that Ballard has been created by God. The book poses the question: If a monstrous man like Ballard is a child of God, then what kind of God controls the universe? McCarthy's tentative answer is that the belief in God as a benevolent force is a false belief. The real nature of God is that he works in violent and mysterious ways that are incomprehensible to people. McCarthy explores this same issue of God's nature as violent and possibly unjust in *The Sunset Limited*, *The Road*, and *The Crossing*. Through these thematic reflections, McCarthy's work reduces the complexity of the human experience to universal, omnipotent forces. He ignores the minute concerns that tend to consume daily human existence in favor of addressing timeless considerations about God and human nature.

The clutter of everyday life does figure into *Suttree*, McCarthy's homage to alcoholism. McCarthy explores self-reliance in the way that Cornelius Suttree ekes out a living on his houseboat. Suttree is inherently good, but his heavy drinking makes him a social outcast who seeks out a place among other outcasts. Unlike McCarthy's earlier Southern gothic novels, society at least is apparent in *Suttree*. The alcoholics in Knoxville are functioning members of society, albeit at the lowest levels. They live, work, steal, go to prison, and are known entities with personal histories. In this work, society has the power to contain the struggle between good and evil.

Society does not function as a form of social control in *Blood Meridian*. In fact, society is virtually nonexistent in this book, which is a philosophical treatise on the nature of war as the ultimate state of existence. In fact, the Judge, the genocidal organizer whose character serves as a brutal arbiter of justice in a world defined by brutality, claims that "War is God." This sentiment reflects McCarthy's most digressive and blasphemous views of God. By taking such a strong stance about the nature of

God, McCarthy posits a deeply unsettling view of humanity—we are born to kill and be killed—and all other trades, arts, and beliefs must succumb to this reality.

GOOD VERSUS EVIL

McCarthy's exploration of good and evil plays a secondary role in his lengthy exploration of destiny versus human will in The Border Trilogy. For the first time in these three books, McCarthy's male protagonists are inherently good and innocent. Their struggle is to maintain their innocence in a fallen world. They are resourceful and resilient, but ultimately they are defeated by the world. Yet, they maintain their goodness throughout their struggles. In this way, McCarthy adds to his exploration of the nature of good and evil. Through the survival of his male protagonists, McCarthy suggests that, although the world be a fallen place, a place that is capable of destroying good people, goodness and beauty will survive. McCarthy transfers this idea of goodness and beauty persisting on the individual level to the societal level in the novel he publishes after The Border Trilogy—No Country for Old Men. In this latter book, Sheriff Bell's earthy philosophical musings about the nature of humanity and human society cast the drug trade not just as a matter of criminality but as a struggle for civilization itself.

Through his body of work, McCarthy revisits the notion that human nature is eternal and the power of society to change that nature is almost nonexistent. It is this view—his version of nature over nurture—that has earned McCarthy a label as a "conservative" thinker. He also presents to his readers a worldview in which society is represented as tremendously fragile. Through this worldview, he considers the fact that social forces are not as powerful as many in the baby boomer generation have suggested. In fact, society is inherently vulnerable to the actions of a few people. In No Country for Old Men, McCarthy explores society's vulnerability to the destructive forces inherent in human nature using the drug trade as the cause of conflict.

The drug dealers are all anonymous, ahistoric characters who are playing a zero-sum game. From McCarthy's perspective, this is a terrifying prospect. To perpetuate their livelihood, they are willing to destroy everything or to be completely destroyed in the process. This total embrace of corrosiveness is a fundamental change in the social fabric that makes the novel relevant.

McCarthy's work exhibits two points of view on drugs. The socially acceptable drug, alcohol, is portrayed as being socially corrosive, but there is a whiff of romantic rebellion in the characters that inhabit Knoxville. In *No Country for Old Men*, the drug trade along the U.S.-Mexico border consumes everyone in and around the drug trade. Interestingly, this book does not portray the actual effects of drug abuse on individuals, in contrast to *Suttree*, in which the effects of alcohol addiction receive personal treatment. McCarthy portrays the drug trade as an environment that fosters the most destructive human characteristics—violence and remorselessness.

Both characteristics are fully expressed in *No Country for Old Men* through the character of Anton Chigurh. McCarthy imbues Chigurh with some noble traits, however. McCarthy provides some insight into the reason behind Chigurh's dual nature: In an interview in which he discussed the book, McCarthy said he has known some drug dealers who are lovely and gracious, but they understand that every day someone is probably trying to kill them. In an echo of that tense existence, Chigurh says that he is "an expert in a very difficult field" (p. 251–252). Chigurh functions as a foil to Llewellyn Moss, who tries to become an expert in this "difficult field." Moss, however, does not possess Chigurh's sadism or ruthlessness, which, consequently, dooms him to failure.

In *No Country for Old Men*, McCarthy makes a clear distinction between the negative effects of alcohol and drug abuse: From his perspective, drugs destroy society whereas alcohol destroys the individual. McCarthy suggests that the drug trade is so greedy, violent, and corrupt that it overwhelms the general optimism of our culture writ large. In *No Country for Old Men*, McCarthy portrays a world in which the power of these negative forces paralyzes the justice-wielding elements of contemporary society, which has chosen to ignore the high-stakes nature of this struggle between good and evil. It is no coincidence that the nihilism of the drug trade eclipses the morality of Sheriff Bell, another of McCarthy's self-reliant heroes. By contrasting self-reliance with the more dangerous aspects of human nature, McCarthy suggests that people do not understand the world as it really is, and thus they end up in a state of cosmic despair. Thus cultural nihilism begets ennui, which, in the end, will be civilization's downfall. Understood in this way, the violence of the drug trade is another manifestation of McCarthy's pessimism about the cosmic state of human morality.

Violence and Destruction

In his latest novel, *The Road*, McCarthy taps into social anxiety about this end of civilization in a way that separates this later work from earlier publications. One of the most enduring elements of this novel is its representation of total environmental collapse. The destroyed world he renders in the book developed from conversations McCarthy had with a number of scientists about nuclear winter. (McCarthy is a fellow at the Santa Fe Institute, a nonprofit think tank in New Mexico. He is the only writer on fellowship with SFI.) Cultural anxiety about nuclear war has become commonplace in the postnuclear age; however, in the modern era, this anxiety has taken a different form in that the origins of such an attack, or even an environmental catastrophe, are much more difficult to pinpoint. This uncertainty is perhaps why McCarthy never explains the origins of the environmental collapse in *The Road*. McCarthy addresses an issue—the end of the world—that is as old as humanity but does so in a topical way that makes readers consider the results of environmental collapse rather than its causes.

McCarthy's novel reflects the belief that the strength of human influence on the natural world has become unsettlingly apparent. The extreme bleakness of *The Road* is a cautionary tale about environmental degradation. It is also a clear reminder of McCarthy's pessimistic philosophy about human destiny: The vast majority of us are ignorant, selfish fools who suffer from an inherently destructive nature that, in all probability, will result in our collective destruction—just as we have collectively ravaged the natural world.

The same dangerous human impulses that McCarthy has explored throughout his body of work—the compulsion toward violence that flourishes beyond the reach of social structures—is explored as a zero-sum game in *The Road*, where people are brutalized in a world absent of culture and must do anything to survive. In this book, McCarthy posits the possibility of a kind of global nihilism as the destiny of humanity. As an antidote to the bleakness of McCarthy's worldview, readers should remember the inherent romanticism of many of McCarthy's later characters, who struggle to maintain their inherently good nature despite existing within cultures that destroy the good, ethical individual. In *The Road*, arguably McCarthy's most bleak work to date, the two protagonists are inherently good. That goodness is the crucial thread to hold onto when considering McCarthy's exploration of the continuing moral problem of violence in today's world. McCarthy encourages his readers to consider that evil violence is inevitable and will never be defeated—and may even be the predominant element of human nature—but that such a thing as noble violence can counter evil brutality.

It is the permanence of this dynamic that puts McCarthy philosophically at odds with modern culture, whose various political movements, religions, and social organization have at the center of their collective unconscious the gradual improvement of humanity. McCarthy's work suggests that he is deeply pessimistic about any attempt to permanently "improve" humanity.

Despite his pessimism about human nature, McCarthy represents a tradition in literature that reaches back to Homer and other icons of classical literature in that he understands the importance of telling a good story. In short, through the very act of writing, McCarthy embraces the belief that literature has a crucial social function that expands the education of a culture and an individual beyond the traditional venues of school and church and family. Interestingly, McCarthy's novels, which draw on the whole of Western knowledge—both humanistic and scientific, are becoming accepted by mainstream Americans at a time when anti-intellectualism is rampant. (For example, a 2008 editorial by *New York Times* writer Nicholas D. Kristof cited a poll that found that "Americans are as likely to believe in flying saucers as in evolution.")

McCarthy's work reflects humanity's hostility toward rationalism. This widespread ignorance is part of the reason for his bleak worldview, which is evident in his work from early novels like *Child of God*, in which Lester Ballard demonstrates a painful lack of intellectual curiosity during a poignant encounter with a blacksmith, to his last novel, *The Road*, in which the most important trade human beings can master is cannibalism.

Given the violence, depravity, and pessimism evident in McCarthy's work, it might seem odd to suggest that he values civilization. Yet, his romantic male protagonists intuit and recognize that there is beauty in the world, and in this way, McCarthy's work stands for an enduring vision about the transcendental importance of human existence. First, he acknowledges that suffering is an elemental component of life that should not necessarily be evidence of God's indifference or malevolence. In fact, suffering brings out greatness of character, which echoes a classical view of humanity (for example, consider the suffering Odysseus endures in Homer's classic work). His coupling of suffering with environmental collapse in *The Road* is a straightforward example of how McCarthy interweaves contemporary issues with classical themes. Yet, he began developing this multilayered thematic approach in his early works.

His environmental ethos as it pertains to his historical interest in the Southern pastoral, wilderness preservation, and environmental collapse forms a prophetic nexus against the excessive destruction of nature by human. His message about the importance of nature to civilization is beautifully distilled in the lyrical passage about the brook trout at the end of *The Road*, whose extinction is "a thing which could not be put back" (p. 241).

If it is our destiny to destroy ourselves, then the very enterprise of all human knowledge can be called into question. In fact, McCarthy powerfully renders this doubt about knowledge when *The Road*'s unnamed protagonist stands in a library and experiences "some rage" at all the lies contained within all the books in the library. This anger is not rage at anti-intellectualism, but rather it is anger against the result of the hubris that is part and parcel of the anti-intellectualism that in the beginning of the twenty-first century has strong currency in our culture. It is rage at the destruction of civilization, rage at the brave new world where the knowledge amassed over the ages is reduced to ash.

In contemporary society, environmental issues are frequently cast in the vein of political ideology—liberal versus conservative—instead of in a more pragmatic way. McCarthy's novels, particularly *No Country for Old Men* and *The Road* have value in that they strip away the ideology surrounding political debates to show that there is a transcendent struggle going on the for the well-being of humanity that is wholly independent of political affiliation.

McCarthy's iconoclastic individualism is a common theme of the quintessentially American character, a quality that Americans have always admired. McCarthy's works reconnect his readers to the American ideal of self-reliance. When Sheriff EdTom Bell in *No Country* passes judgment on the nature of his own character in comparison against "the old-timers" (sheriffs who have preceded him as arbiters of justice in that part of Texas), it is easy to see him as hearkening back to a time when things were better or simpler. However, McCarthy's invocation of nostalgia encourages readers to remember the virtues of the past so that they can be incorporated into the present.

But even the character's nostalgic recollections are colored by an understanding of the pessimistic view that the world is filled with struggle and misunderstanding. When Bell recounts an episode from his military service, he reveals that he was rewarded for an act of bravery that in his mind's eye was not worthy of a hero's accolade. Through Bell, McCarthy clearly says that there was no golden era that is lost and can never be recovered; he is saying that each generation has to discover the virtues that have enabled civilization to survive. This is a problem as old as humanity itself. Furthermore, Bell's friend cautions the Sheriff that his anxieties about a fundamental change occurring in society are a sign of "vanity." What interesting advice, particularly given that in the early twenty-first century, many members of society think that the problems that we collectively face are "new." Thus, the crux of McCarthy's message in his works is that while the problems are new, their cause, the inherent self-destructive aspect of humanity, is as old as human history.

Perhaps more than anything, through the violence and destruction inherent in his works, McCarthy, as a writer and artist, has chosen to perform an ancient role for society. The idea that literature, as an art form, has a public function that goes beyond entertainment and consumption is a crucial one for modern audiences to understand. This ancient idea gets its clearest articulation in Aristotle's poetics, wherein he describes the importance of catharsis. Art is necessary for purging negative emotions. Therefore, although some may see the nihilism in McCarthy's novels as decadent and unnecessary, it offers the chance for modern audiences to confront unspoken anxieties without having to experience firsthand the human suffering and social collapse inherent in his works.

DISCUSSION QUESTIONS

- Do you think McCarthy's work is political?
- What are the drawbacks of thinking about environmental collapse from a political perspective?
- How do McCarthy's works comment on contemporary issues?
- Why do you think McCarthy portrays drinking as less dangerous than using narcotics?
- Why is violence an inevitable part of human existence?
- Why do you think McCarthy likes to associate with scientists instead of writers?

15

POP CULTURE IN CORMAC McCARTHY'S WORK

Culture is the knowledge shared by members of a social organization (Eitzen and Zinn, 107). In their work on understanding social constructs, Eitzen and Zinn identify six types of shared knowledge that constitute culture: symbols, technology, ideologies, norms, values, and roles. Popular culture, then, expands this shared knowledge using contemporary forms to express those six types of knowledge. Today, for example, popular culture reinforces society's shared knowledge through music, film, the media, clothing styles, and language. In general, pop culture consists of ideas, experiences, material goods, and language that permeate much of society at a particular time in history.

As a contemporary author, Cormac McCarthy is notable for a virtually universal omission of any reference to popular culture in his published works. McCarthy creates landscapes, characters, and plots that are almost completely stripped of any contextual reference to pop culture. His characters do not drive Chevys; they drive pick-up trucks. They do not drink Budweiser; they drink beer. There is one reference to Coca-Cola in *The Road*. Apart from that, there are almost no references to the material trappings that define contemporary American society—for example, clothing, music, television, an obsession with celebrity, and rampant consumerism. And with the exception of the occasional curse word, even his characters' speech avoids using any of the slang that has become ubiquitous.

The lack of popular culture references in his published work is a deliberate stylistic technique McCarthy uses to render the epic scope and allegorical nature of his subject matter. Most of McCarthy's work addresses issues pertaining to the universal human condition, not society. His characters are not structured as worldly creatures with a developed awareness of being active participants of an extended social group. To the contrary, with the exception of Sheriff Bell in *No Country for Old Men*, Black in *The Sunset Limited*, and the Telfairs in *The Stonemason*, almost all of McCarthy's male protagonists live in relative isolation, far removed from society's grasp. Popular culture is not in their purview. As a result of this epic scope and allegorical nature, Cormac McCarthy's novels do not easily lend themselves to film adaptations. However, several of McCarthy's books have been rendered as screenplays, each with differing levels of success.

ALL THE PRETTY HORSES (RELEASED 2000)

The first of McCarthy's books to be made into a screenplay for film was *All the Pretty Horses*. Released in 2000 with an ensemble of A-list Hollywood actors, the film fared poorly at the box office. The screenplay was adapted by Ted Tally, a well-known Hollywood writer with extensive experience adapting novels to film. His best known work is the screenplay adaptation of *Silence of the Lambs*.

Expectations for the film version of *All the Pretty Horses* were high. The movie was directed by Billy Bob Thornton, who won an Academy Award in 1996 for *Sling Blade*, a film he wrote, directed, and played the lead in. The role of John Grady Cole was played by Matt Damon, and Penelope Cruz played the role of Alejandra. But it is the young Lucas Black, who first worked with Thornton on *Sling Blade* and was cast as Jimmy Blevins, who delivers the best performance in the movie.

Critics almost universally panned the film, delivering negative critiques of the lead actors' performance, the score, the directing, and the editing. Thornton and Damon claimed that the film's producer, after seeing a preliminary cut of the movie, required that Thornton cut one-third of the content for release.

Despite the movie's numerous flaws, Black's performance as Jimmy Blevins is memorable. He is funny, desperate, murderous, and haunting. His performance, however, is not enough to overcome the anemic rendering of the relationship between Cole and Alejandra. In fact, the film does a remarkably poor job of capturing the lyrical and philosophical passion of the story, embodied by Cole's love affair with horses and with Alejandra. Both are glossed over too quickly to foster any meaningful thematic development. The problems seem to be with Tally's screenplay and Thornton's directing, which renders Cole's passion as ephemeral images of herds of wild horses stampeding at night, as well as with the lack of chemistry between the actors playing Cole and Alejandra.

In addition to these narrative and lyrical problems, the musical score detracts from instead of enhances the movie. The problem is a clash of pop culture ideology with McCarthy's unadorned story. The score tries for something that approximates modern Western music, but this is at odds with the novel, which articulates a melancholy story about young men pursuing an anachronistic dream of living as ranch hands at a time in history when that is no longer possible. The score does not register the futility that is an essential component of the characters' journey into and out of Mexico. Instead, the score features a ridiculous swelling of strings that accompanies Cole, Blevins, and Rawlins as they cross the Rio Grande into Mexico, whooping as they go.

Nowhere is this disconnect between the style in the original novel and the film rendition more apparent than in the movie version of Cole's knife fight while in a Mexican prison. In the movie version, dozens of inmates silently and passively bear witness to the life-or-death battle between Cole and the *cuchillero* (an assassin who kills with a knife). The knife fight in the book is dramatic and ends with Cole barely escaping death by stabbing his attacker in the chest with a single fatal blow. In the movie, Cole flies into a fury like a typical Hollywood action hero and easily vanquishes the *cuchillero*.

In the book, McCarthy sets up this last battle by describing how Cole and Rawlins spend several days fighting for their lives in the open yard of the penitentiary. These brutal turf wars lead to the final lengthy confrontation between Cole and the *cuchillero*. This fight takes place in the empty mess hall, and the *cuchillero* inflicts a host of injuries on Cole. He spends many days recovering in the prison infirmary. Cole kills the *cuchillero*, and the movie relays this information to viewers during an unbearably maudlin scene of an inmate singing after his death. This gesture suggests some kind of collective or shared mourning among the inmates. It clashes with the book's sentiments, which describe a sadistic prison population totally devoid of sentiment in which Cole and Rawlins are prey.

The screenplay invents another, similarly odd episode when Cole calls Alejandra on the phone. Throughout the conversation, the shot features a man, presumably mentally disturbed, who is dancing a jig while

Cole tries to persuade his former lover to meet him in the city. The film-makers juxtapose this moment of painful romantic yearning with a contrived symbol of madness. The effect rings hollow. Instead of leaning on McCarthy's reductive style to convey meaning and create a mood, the movie relies on heavy-handed artistic symbolism.

Furthermore, the seriousness of the lamentation for a lost way of life, as a cowboy and ranch hand, is undercut by this superficial aesthetic. What is also unfortunate is that the role of Alejandra's aunt is completely unrealized in the screenplay. This results in a narrative deficiency that ignores McCarthy's crucial juxtaposition of the failed Mexican Revolution with the encroachment of modernity as a backdrop to the story. Instead of providing appropriate cinematic representation of these important subjects, the film renders what could have been a memorable story about the loss of a way of life as a Western soap opera. The movie also ignores all of McCarthy's references to the Comanche Indian. In fact, the film has expunged Mexican history, Indian history, and American history, reducing the story to a bare bones narrative in which the most memorable image is that of the glaring whiteness of the actors' teeth.

OUTER DARK (PREVIEWED 2005)

The second of McCarthy's novels to be adapted to film is *Outer Dark*. The film has been written, produced, and directed by an independent filmmaker named Stephen Imwalle. Imwalle has been working on the movie since at least 2005. He showed an excerpt from the film at the annual gathering of the Cormac McCarthy Society in 2005, but since then, there has been no confirmed release date for the movie, nor has there been any information about a public screening of the film in its entirety.

NO COUNTRY FOR OLD MEN (RELEASED 2007)

In November 2007, the writer-director team, brothers Joel and Ethan Coen, released their movie version of *No Country for Old Men*. In 2008, this third adaptation of a McCarthy novel to screen won four Oscars, including for best picture, best directing, best acting, and best screenplay adaptation.

McCarthy's involvement with the first two adaptations of his novel was virtually absent, but *No Country for Old Men* was a different story. McCarthy clearly admires the Coen brothers' work, which includes quirky, dark comedies like *Fargo, Raising Arizona,* and *The Big*

Lebowski, as well as more serious dramatic fare such as *Miller's Crossing* and *Barton Fink*. McCarthy's respect for the Coen brothers runs deep enough that on the eve of the movie's release, the notorious recluse participated in an interview with the Coen brothers for *Time* magazine.

McCarthy's public endorsement of the Coen brothers' film may stem from the fact that the screenplay adaptation remained true to the novel with only a few minor variations. In addition, the film was a commercial and critical success. Part of the Coen brothers' success in executing the first well-rendered adaptation of a McCarthy novel relates directly to the nature of the book. It is one of the first novels McCarthy has written in which the scope of the philosophical and historical territory is relatively constrained by place and time. In addition the driver of the story's action—the drug trade across the U.S.-Mexico border—is a subject that has permeated popular culture, particularly through Hollywood. Film representations of the drug trade have a long history stretching back to the *French Connection* in 1971, which was the first R-rated movie to win the Oscar for best picture. Films like director Steven Soderbergh's *Traffic* (released in 2000) and Ridley Scott's *American Gangster* (2007) have become cultural references for society's knowledge about the drug trade.

One of the main alterations the Coen brothers made to their screenplay was to reduce the philosophical digressions of Sheriff EdTom Bell, played by Tommy Lee Jones. While stream of consciousness is an effective literary device, it does not translate well to film. Sheriff Bell's character as rendered by McCarthy is something of a trope—he is the old man who perceives himself to be at odds with a rapidly changing society. And while he is a stereotype and, as such, not an original character, he confronts challenges with a wry humor and steadfast nature that makes him compelling.

An interesting minor change that the Coens made to the narrative was the insertion of a chase scene involving a dog early in the film. The dog has been set after Moss, played by the actor Josh Brolin, by a couple of anonymous drug dealers who know he stumbled upon a botched drug deal. Moss calmly shoots the animal as it is about to eat him face-first. This encounter does not exist in the book, although Moss does see a dog, and so the episode in the screenplay is not completely without a reference point in the original. The Coen brothers' rendition of this scene is philosophically aligned with McCarthy's animal aesthetic, which is explored in detail in Wallis R. Sanborn's book, *Animals in the Fiction of Cormac McCarthy*. In addition to demonstrating Moss's masculine coolness under extreme pressure, through its death, the dog becomes another empty casualty of the drug trade. Animals and people are universally disposable. They are useful only insofar as they can sustain the trade; their individual being is without value. This is the essential theme the Coens are exploring in their film.

In addition to subtle additions to the screenplay, the directors use scenes in which the characters interact to effectively construct film versions of McCarthy's fictive characters. This is particularly true in the case of the bounty hunter, Wells, played by actor Woody Harrelson. In the book, Wells's motivations and his nature are ambiguous. However, Harrelson's portrayal of Wells is extremely effective. In a memorable scene involving an exchange between him and Moss as Moss is recovering in a Mexican hospital after being shot by Anton Chigurh, the dual nature of both men's characters becomes clear. Neither man is afraid of Chigurh, played by the actor Javier Bardem. Both embody an unusually courageous sense of masculinity. But this masculinity is not chivalrous. Both men imply that they adhere to a loose moral code. This gray area of morality—a hallmark of which is unwaveringly courageous masculinity with no regard for societal convention—reveals a commonality shared by the two characters that is not immediately obvious in the novel.

The film version puts a fine point on the nature of Moss's character through the directors' interpretation of the episode in which Moss picks up a young female hitchhiker. In the book, Moss picks up the young woman, and it is implied that he has no intention of seducing her. But those intentions are not crystal clear. In the film, the Coens eliminate any ambiguity about the nature of their encounter by having the two meet poolside at the hotel where Moss is staying. This provides an additional element of tragedy to his death and the subsequent death of his wife, Carla Jean. Carla Jean dies wondering whether or not her husband was faithful to her. However, both reader and viewer know that Moss did not violate his wedding vows.

As the narrative builds toward a collision between Chigurh and Moss, viewers of the film are primed for a final confrontation between the two that will determine the outcome of the struggle between good and evil. Moss surprises Chigurh in his hotel room, and there is a brief gunfight between the two men. Both men are wounded, but Moss escapes with the money. After eluding Chigurh for several more days, the Mexican drug dealers catch up with Moss and kill him. The rendering of his death is interesting in that, in both film and book, it occurs offstage. In a story filled with violence and gore, Moss's final moments are mysteriously invisible.

Chigurh's final moments in the movie, in comparison, are fully visible. Chigurh, who fancies himself a powerful agent of destiny who eliminates all randomness from life, is driving down a suburban street when he is broadsided at an intersection. He is badly wounded in the crash.

Even though Chigurh survives the car crash, he is not in good shape, and readers and viewers are left to wonder how ably he will survive after the accident. He, like Moss, is a resourceful and durable man, but the accident seems to destroy his own darkly romantic vision of his own purpose and power. This romantic vision is emphasized by the way in which Chigurh affects Sheriff Bell's destiny in the film. In the movie, Chigurh seems to inexplicably spare Bell's life. This moral ambiguity is not evident in the book, where Bell's timing ensures that he narrowly misses encountering Chigurh for the second time, the first being when he arrived at Moss's trailer minutes after Chigurh had left. Despite the slight discrepancy between book and movie, the effect of both instances is similar. Bell's courage protects him from death so that he can contemplate his own mortality and the social and cosmic corrosion that the drug trade has wrought. In addition, Bell survives to confront the moral abyss that the future seems to hold.

Bell's narrow misses with Chigurh highlight his own frailty as well as his own determination in a world he does not understand and in which he does not feel he belongs. The book (but not the movie) echoes this profound alienation by invoking the disappeared Comanche, which McCarthy also does in *All the Pretty Horses*. McCarthy meditates upon the destruction of a heroic, violent, and tragic tribe to provide a foil for Bell's despair. Thus, despair and suffering form the ultimate understanding and experience of the world for Anglo and Comanche alike.

THE ROAD (IN POSTPRODUCTION)

It will be interesting to see whether Chockstone Pictures, the company that is producing *The Road,* will be as successful as the Coen brothers were with their adaptation of *No Country for Old Men. The Road* has been filmed and is in postproduction. It was filmed in Pennsylvania and is slated for release in 2009.

Additional film versions of McCarthy's work could be forthcoming. Tommy Lee Jones, who starred in *No Country for Old Men,* bought the rights to *Blood Meridian.* Industry reports first suggested that Ridley Scott (director of *American Gangster*) agreed to direct this film, but Todd Field has since been identified as the director and writer for the movie adaptation. In 2001, Field received two Oscar nominations for his screenwriting and directorial debut on the film *In the Bedroom.* The directorial change may have to do with *Blood Meridian*'s challenging subject matter—the main feature of the novel is a series of outlandish, grotesque, and brutal massacres.

This history of American violence fascinates readers of McCarthy's work and, indeed, McCarthy himself. Violence pervades American culture in part because of our nation's violent history. This particular aspect of McCarthy's work, his obsession with extreme violence, might be his strongest connection to popular culture. Yet, his interest in violence is deeply rooted in the philosophical themes he explores through his work. Rarely does McCarthy deploy violence with the gratuitousness of popular culture, which uses violence as a vehicle for sales. In fact, the violence in his work is shockingly real and far removed from a lot of the cartoonish violence that dominates its representation in popular culture.

Scholars found this aspect of his work so compelling that one of the first books to be published about McCarthy's writing was called *Sacred Violence*. This book, which included the proceedings of an early academic conference on his works, was reissued in 2002 as a two-volume set. The title suggests that there is an aspect to violence that is not antithetical to a general understanding of violence. For example, McCarthy views violence as an inherent and unavoidable aspect of humanity, whereas contemporary popular culture tends to deplore and to decry it, at least for those members of society who are not actively consuming it. McCarthy is not advocating violence, but he is taking a stance that contradicts the notion in popular culture that believes violence is a social ill that can be "solved." For example, in *Blood Meridian,* the Judge addresses the pointlessness of being concerned with the eradication of violence when he says, of war, that you "might as well ask man what he thinks of stone." Through the character of the Judge, McCarthy suggests that there is no qualitative judgment to be issued about whether war is good or bad or whether human beings can make it go away. Like stone, war is part of the natural landscape human beings inhabit. It always has been and it always will be, *ad infinitum*. Given this view, the disparity between his representation of violence as a cultural force and the depiction of violence in popular culture grows wider. He implies that Americans do not take violence seriously, which is a terrible mistake, because violence is an inherent component of human nature.

Although McCarthy's overarching philosophy about violence is at odds with contemporary society, the use of violence in McCarthy's work does find some common ground with popular culture. For instance, violence is commonly used as a medium to foster male bonding in popular culture—for example, violent video games, films, comic books, and sports are all common tools that young men use to connect with each other. McCarthy, too, uses violence to strengthen the connection between his male characters, particularly in his later works in which relationships between male protagonists are more fully developed than in his Southern gothic novels. The bond forged in the context of violence is evident in the pairings of: the father and son in *The Road*; John Grady Cole, Lacey Rawlins, and Jimmy Blevins in *All the Pretty Horses*; and the brothers Billy and Boyd in *The Crossing*.

The bond between men through violence seems to transcend conventional interpersonal connections. Nowhere is this seen more starkly than in the novel *Blood Meridian*. The scalp hunters are bound to their code of violence, not to each other. This aesthetic directly contrasts the way in which violence is sentimentalized in popular culture.

For much of his career as a writer, McCarthy has been at odds with popular culture; he has existed on the literary margins of relative obscurity. His later books have broadened his appeal and his reputation, firmly ensconcing him as a contributing member of popular culture. This dynamic of popular culture's tendency to assimilate experimental and avant-garde art is a powerful characteristic of contemporary society. McCarthy's work simultaneously appeals to both high culture and mass culture; he is both a pulpy and a classical writer. His work adds to the general understanding of popular culture in that he represents the lives of people, good and bad, who exist at the margins of mainstream society, although the characters may not necessarily perceive or represent themselves in that way. This valorization of the noble outsider is a quintessentially American perspective, one that has been perpetuated by popular culture itself in the form of film, television, comic books, and novels, and in a previous era, radio. The transcendental, self-reliant cowboy, outlaw, or hillbilly is a recurring theme in McCarthy's work. His fascination with the heroic individual ultimately places his work firmly in the mainstream of popular culture.

McCarthy's status as a member of the pop culture mainstream has been ensured by the way in which he and his work have become reference points for other working artists. For example, Nick Cave, the Australian artist who is primarily known for his work as a singer/songwriter with the group Nick Cave and the Bad Seeds, published his first novel in 1989. The book, titled *And the Ass Saw the Angel*, owes a particular debt to McCarthy's Southern gothic aesthetic insofar as it features an imbecile, a debased atmosphere, and extreme psychological and physical violence. Cave also has a connection to John Hillcoat, the Australian director of *The Road*. Cave and Hillcoat cowrote the screenplay for the Australian movie *The Proposition*.

The Road, as well, which Hillcoat finished filming in May 2008, has become imbued with pop culture reference points. The cast and crew of the movie have talked about their Australian connection to the Mad Max series and have acknowledged that McCarthy's apocalyptic vision is quite different than that depicted through the futuristic tenor of the famous Mad Max trilogy.

Even though McCarthy imbues his stories with virtually no elements from popular culture, the material itself lends itself to representation in the popular media. The film adaptations of his books have brought McCarthy's vision and philosophy into full view for mainstream society. McCarthy's work reflects few influences from popular culture itself, but he and his stories have affected contemporary society's own self-knowledge.

DISCUSSION QUESTIONS

- Why is it difficult to successfully make a cinematic adaptation of McCarthy's novels?
- How does the seriousness of McCarthy's works contrast with other popular movies and shows?
- What is the difference between violence in other popular works and violence in McCarthy's movies?
- If McCarthy is at odds with popular culture, why do so many people like his novels and movies?
- What is the significance of McCarthy avoiding popular culture in his works?

16

CORMAC McCARTHY
ON THE INTERNET

Type the words "Cormac McCarthy" into the Google search bar and the search engine will return somewhat less than 1.5 million hits. A quick scan of the results reveals that, like many Web searches, a number of the hits pull from the same Web sites. A cursory exploration of those sites that are original reveals that much of the information contained on them is culled from a handful of online resources that publish reliable, current, and relevant information about the writer and his work.

This chapter will provide a brief analysis of the most comprehensive and regularly maintained sites dedicated to McCarthy and his books: http://www.cormacmccarthy.com, his Wikipedia page at http://en.wiki pedia.org/wiki/Cormac_McCarthy, and http://www.JohnSepich.com. The rest of this section will assess other popular and independent sites that contain credible and interesting information about McCarthy's life and works.

THE CORMAC MCCARTHY SOCIETY WEB SITE

For scholars and interested lay readers of McCarthy's work, the most comprehensive and informative Web site is http://www.cormacmccarthy. com. This is the official Web site of the Cormac McCarthy Society, an independent organization of academics and casual readers. The group began informally in 1993 at an academic conference about McCarthy's works held at Bellarmine College in Kentucky and evolved into a non-profit education organization that hosts an annual conference in the fall and participates in panel discussions at the annual meeting of the American Literature Association. Several of the society's founding members have been championing his works for decades. Their expertise and objectivity makes this the most credible and well-maintained online resource about McCarthy's writings. Virtually all of the information on the Web site has been peer-reviewed, which is rarely the case with other sites.

The society has its own online journal, which is only available to subscribers. The articles in the online journal assume a fairly substantial knowledge of literary history. The 2005 edition of the online journal is now available in print through academic libraries and features many fine articles on *No Country for Old Men*. For readers and scholars who are interested in gaining exposure to the current state of scholarship about McCarthy, the society's online journal is a valuable resource and is well-worth the modest annual membership fee of $35 ($25 for students and members of the U.S. military).

Membership in the society provides participatory access to the forum, an online discussion group for McCarthy readers. The forum provides a space for casual, intellectual exchange about the author's works and balances the site's more scholarly material. While the society's Web site is not updated as regularly as the Wikipedia page on Cormac McCarthy, it contains crucial biographical information and the most comprehensive bibliography about publications relevant to the author's works.

The site does have a few minor flaws, including haphazard site maintenance. When the site was originally launched, it kept close track of all published articles about McCarthy and his works. The Web site's entry for its own bibliography is imprecise. As of early 2009, the link to the bibliography claims that it has not been updated since 2002; however, clicking on the link reveals that it was updated in 2007. In addition, information about the society's European conference, which is slated to be held every other year, identifies the next tentative date for a European meeting as 2005.

The main weakness of the site's bibliography is that it does not list many of the current reviews that have been published about McCarthy's work. Understandably, scholarly and consumer interest in McCarthy's work has exploded and resulted in a plethora of print and Web-based reviews of his work. In 1994, two years after McCarthy's first commercial success with *All the Pretty Horses*, one person could have easily read almost everything that had been written about the author. Today, that is not a practical enterprise as new books, articles, scholarship, and reviews are found in the most disparate of places. However, Dianne Luce, the McCarthy scholar who updates the bibliography on the society's Web site, has compiled the most comprehensive bibliography available of publications about the author and his works. The bibliography, which includes both academic and consumer publications, is organized by medium into the following seven categories: scholarly studies, dissertations, theses, interviews with the author, reviews (organized by author's works), news articles and journalism (organized chronologically), and references in interviews and writing by other authors.

The organization of these categories is helpful to those doing research. For example, the reviews are organized by book, and the news articles and journalism section is organized by decade. While it may take some time to find a particular article, this information constitutes the most comprehensive online bibliography of McCarthy and his works. Virtually all of the information on McCarthy that exists online can be traced back to this Web site.

THE CORMAC MCCARTHY WIKIPEDIA PAGE

Although the society's Web site is the most thorough and comprehensive online resource for information about McCarthy and his writing, perhaps the most accessible starting point for beginning McCarthy scholars or those with a casual interest in the author and his body of work is Wikipedia. Although the notes section and the external links section on McCarthy's page do not capture the richness of secondary writing that exists on McCarthy, this site provides the most essential information about McCarthy in a manner that is accessible and easily comprehensible for beginning students. Particularly in the realm of film adaptations, McCarthy's page on Wikipedia is the most regularly updated site for people who are interested in tracking information on the movie-making progress. The Wikipedia moderators' strongest section on the Web site is the biographical section. Many other sites have good information on McCarthy, but, as has been the case since the beginning of his career, the best information on McCarthy is compiled and maintained by a dedicated cadre of fans and scholars.

THE CORMAC MCCARTHY ONLINE CONCORDANCE

The type of devotion McCarthy receives is notable in the work of one McCarthy scholar in particular, John Sepich. Sepich's book, *Notes on Blood Meridian*, made him well-known in the coterie of McCarthy scholars. The book was originally published in 1993 by Bellarmine College Press and went out of print a few years later, driving the price for first editions into the stratosphere, as much as $800. When working on my dissertation, I purchased the book for $12.50 in Von's bookstore in West Lafayette, Indiana; since Sepich's new edition was published in 2008, first editions now sell for $250 to $500.

His book is a scholarly classic. Sepich, along with Christopher Forbis and Wesley Morgan, have developed an online concordance to the works of McCarthy (http://www.JohnSepich.com). The quirky site, which also includes detailed instructions on how to construct utilitarian household items that Sepich has dubbed "horse barn inventions," is a unique resource for individuals who are interested in studying the language that McCarthy uses.

The Web site reveals a fondness for and devotion to McCarthy's work. One of the most prominent features of McCarthy's writing is his vocabulary and the prose styles in which he has employed his encyclopedic knowledge over the course of his novels. This concordance is an original and elaborate resource for understanding the author's talent for dialect and his prodigious vocabulary.

The concordances show the frequency of words throughout the author's whole oeuvre. There are links that list words unique to McCarthy's novels. This is a useful resource for both the most advanced scholars as well as undergraduate or high school students who are interested in working on McCarthy. The resource is comprehensive and can be searched by novel or by word. For example, if someone is interested in researching McCarthy's use of mountains, one could scroll the index for the word "mountain" and see what pages in which novel that McCarthy uses that word.

OTHER CORMAC MCCARTHY INFORMATION ONLINE

The three Web sites discussed thus far provide the bulk of relevant and authoritative information about McCarthy and his career. Other Web sites, however, while not crucial to McCarthy scholarship, do provide additional information about the author and his works. For example, a movie on YouTube called "Searching for Cormac" chronicles two young men, fans of McCarthy's writing, as they travel around the Southwest trying to unearth the notoriously reclusive author. Tracking him down is a minor trope in McCarthy lore insofar as many journalists and scholars lament the difficulty they faced in trying to locate and interview him while noting his utter reticence at the prospect of being found.

One of the more interesting scenes from the YouTube clip features the two men as they try to persuade a librarian at a library the author is known to frequent to share information about him. The ironies here are multilayered—in this ridiculous age of celebrity, these two young men have achieved a level of Internet fame because of the author's aversion to his own celebrity status. The clip is one of many examples of the grotesque celebrity-gawking promulgated by the Web on which information has become virtually irrelevant. Other examples include bogus profile pages posted to social networking sites such as MySpace and Facebook by the author's fans. From one perspective, the YouTube video functions as a quaint home movie that is relatively harmless. Its persistence illustrates a lack of respect for the author's oft-expressed desire for privacy, and as such, its very existence demonstrates the selfish motivations of the videographers.

One mainstream Web site that is useful for those with an interest in McCarthy and his work is the *Time* magazine site (http://www.time.com), in particular its archival section. *Time*'s online archives provide instant access to historic reviews of McCarthy's publications, for example, an anonymous 1968 review of *Outer Dark* that is not widely available. The site also contains extensive reviews of *All the Pretty Horses* and *Cities of the Plain*. And although it is only one page long, the *Time* magazine piece in which the Coens and McCarthy interview each other is available on the site and provides important insight into McCarthy's interest in Hollywood and his knowledge of the Coen brothers' work.

Another mainstream site through which contemporary reviews of McCarthy's work can be accessed is the *New York Times Book Review* (http://www.nytimes.com). The site does not provide an exhaustive list of McCarthy's work; however, all of the reviews that can be accessed online are of high quality, and most of these reviews and articles can be accessed without paying a subscription fee. Publisher sites that have review materials, such as Knopf and Random House, are good as well, but because they have distributed McCarthy's work, the variety of reviews that are available about his novels is not as diverse as in the *Times'* book review. The *Times* also published an obscure article about the "Suttree Stagger" (accessed May 8, 2008), which can be found on the site. Although brief, it mentions that McCarthy is "revered" in Knoxville and that there is an event described as a "seven-hour literary pub crawl," which commemorates the spirit and actual locations of McCarthy's Knoxville novel, *Suttree.*

In terms of Web sites dedicated to film adaptations of McCarthy's books, the Internet Movie Database (http://www.imdb.com) is a reliable source for information about these films, including those that are in production, those that have been distributed, and those that are in the early planning stages. As more of McCarthy's books are adapted to the screen, expect this Web site to continue to be the primary source for reliable and up-to-date information about the movies' status. Some useful features of this Web site are the filmography links to actors who are in the movies. Also, links are included to fan reviews, synopses, awards, directors, genre, and film trivia. For example, the page for *No Country for Old Men* includes original information about the making of the film. From the trivia link (accessed May 7, 2008), there is a note about how the screenwriter/director team of Joel and Ethan Coen had to stop filming for a day because of a huge cloud of black smoke that hung in the air. Apparently the film crew for the movie *There Will Be Blood* was testing some pyrotechnics for a scene involving a burning oil derrick, and the result was enough to prevent the Coens from shooting for an entire day.

Other Web sites, such as http://www.popsubculture.com (accessed on May 8, 2008), look promising as sources of previously unearthed information, but most turn out to have culled their information from existing sites. A quick tour of http://www.popsubculture.com reveals dead links and redundant information. This is unfortunate because some links sound quite interesting. One in particular purportedly connects to the alumni academic hall of fame at the University of Tennessee, implying McCarthy had at least a Web presence at the university (this was a dead link). The community weblog hosted by the site metafilter is not that relevant for readers of McCarthy. A fair number of people share thoughts and feelings about McCarthy's novels, but the comments tend toward the general and vague, and ultimately do not make for insightful reading.

Another prominent Web site that maintains reviews of McCarthy's books and movies is http://www.salon.com. Salon is interesting because a detailed search for reviews about McCarthy's work will produce results that advocate dissenting views (for example, see the December 25, 2000, review of the film adaptation of *All the Pretty Horses*, a book that Salon contributing writer Charles Taylor refers to as "one of the more successful literary snow jobs of our time").

Of special interest is Oprah Winfrey's Web site. Oprah selected *The Road* to be part of her book club in 2008. To promote the novel, McCarthy granted an interview to Oprah, which was held at the Santa Fe Institute. This interview is the most substantial that McCarthy has ever given. To see the interview, which only can be viewed on Oprah's site, it is necessary to become a member of Oprah's Book Club.

The book club Web site supports a number of resources for general readers. By searching for *The Road* on her book club link, there are several links of interest. In addition to the aforementioned interview, there are other sections geared toward new and general readers. These links feature themes in the novel, novel excerpts, discussion questions, and a brief biographical section on McCarthy. Oprah's attention to McCarthy is compelling in that it connects today's readers with their parents in appreciation of his work.

The Internet provides a forum for McCarthy readers who are critical of his entire oeuvre or of individual works. Although the books and the scholarly articles do not necessarily advocate appreciation, their content tends to be implicitly if not overtly approving of his work. Now that McCarthy's work is part of the mainstream, it is likely that a wider range of reactions will be registered for and against his work.

For several decades, the reception of McCarthy's work was dominated by a handful of academics. While that group is still dominant in forming the reception of McCarthy's works, access to the Internet is broadening this discussion. Depending on how one views the content of the Internet, this can be either very good or very bad or anywhere along that spectrum. Scholarly criticism will still be paramount in understanding McCarthy's work. Scholarly books are heavily vetted in terms of factual and bibliographic accuracy; Internet postings range from the well informed to uninformed and careless. Thus, these online forums show how the discussion of literary works has been wrested away from scholars; yet, it is refreshing in a way, to see that interpretive gap—the popular and the academic—bridged by the Internet. This process is good for McCarthy's readers, and will ultimately make the level of discussion about his work continually relevant.

DISCUSSION QUESTIONS

- How do these Web sites contribute to a popular understanding of the author and his works?
- What do you think of independent Internet sources such as the "Searching for Cormac" video on YouTube?
- Based on the content of http://www.cormacmccarthy.com, would you consider joining the Cormac McCarthy Society?
- What do you think of Cormac McCarthy not wanting to be associated with his own society in any way?
- What do you think of Oprah's interview with McCarthy?
- Which Web site discussed in this chapter is most useful or interesting?
- What information can you find on http://www.imdb.com that updates information in this book?

17

CORMAC McCARTHY
AND THE MEDIA

For decades, the nature of McCarthy's relationship with the media—print and broadcast—was, if not overtly antagonistic certainly marked by disdain. Over the course of more than thirty years, from the early stages of his writing career in the 1960s into the 1990s, he granted only a handful of very brief interviews to minor publications in Tennessee. Although he did give one minor interview in the 1980s to Mark Morrow for his book *Images of the Southern Writer*, McCarthy agreed to do so reluctantly and only after the persuasive efforts of his original book editor, Erskine Caldwell. He did not sit for his first interview with a nationally distributed publication until 1992.

In the 1960s, 1970s, and 1980s, McCarthy's relationship with the media consisted solely of book reviews. (The titles and locations of these reviews are all listed on http://www.cormacmccarthy.com.) All of his novels received reviews in a variety of popular and academic publications and the critiques were, in general, favorable. Before *All the Pretty Horses*, McCarthy's novels garnered, on average, twenty reviews apiece. After McCarthy won The National Book Award for *All the Pretty Horses*, the number of reviews per novel increased substantially. The most fascinating thing about the history of these reviews is that twenty-three reviews were written for *Blood Meridian*. *Blood Meridian* is arguably McCarthy's greatest work, and, as discussed earlier, it was virtually unread upon publication.

One interesting and midcareer review was Don Williams's piece in the *Chattahoochee Review*. Published in the summer 1993 issue, Williams's review identified McCarthy's small but dedicated group of readers that existed before his first nationally successful novel, *All the Pretty Horses*. After the publication of that novel, according to Williams, a significant number of popular reviews began to register criticism of McCarthy's vision. Much of Williams's review draws on an interview that he conducted with Anne DeLisle, McCarthy's second wife. This interview supplies crucial details that framed popular understanding of the author's life during the middle years of his career.

In 1992, McCarthy sat for an interview with journalist Richard Woodward, which ran in the April 19, 1992, *New York Times Book Review*. The publication of this piece substantially altered McCarthy's relationship with the media. Woodward's interview promoted *All the Pretty Horses* and the next installment in the Border Trilogy, *The Crossing*, and brought a level of exposure to the author that he had never before experienced. Apparently, that was enough to send him running for the hills, because he did not grant another interview for thirteen years, when he sat down again with Woodward in 2005. This time, the interview was published by *Vanity Fair* and was a promotional vehicle for *No Country for Old Men*. The interview, titled "Cormac Country," features the following excerpt:

> Cormac McCarthy would rather hang out with physicists than other writers. He doesn't do blurbs, book tours, or even Oprah. But with the publication of his blood-spattered new novel, No Country for Old Men, he gives his first interview in 13 years—since All the Pretty Horses turned him from cult figure into literary star.

Woodward must have been looking into his oracle's glass because three years later, Oprah Winfrey scored one of her biggest coups when she secured an interview with Cormac McCarthy. The exclusive interview aired on June 5, 2007, and ran for the duration of the program. Since then, McCarthy has become less reclusive and has granted brief but important interviews to the Coen Brothers in *Time* magazine and to *Rolling Stone*, where his name appeared on a cover banner on the December 27, 2007, issue.

McCarthy's interview with Oprah is the most substantial one the author has ever given. Not only is it the most wide ranging, it is the only one that has been televised. The interview was a major accomplishment for Oprah, who incorporated *The Road* into her well-known and heavily promoted Book Club. McCarthy's decision to become a participating author in her book club is an interesting one—by bringing *The Road* into Oprah's purview, McCarthy bridges the divide between popular and scholarly readers. His decision to be interviewed by Oprah was crucial in terms of making his work accessible to as many people as possible. Many academics and some artists shun Oprah's Book Club because of its connection to popular culture. For example, author Jonathan Franzen famously rejected Oprah's invitation to promote his novel *The Corrections* through her book club because of the supposedly middlebrow connotation that goes with such an appearance. McCarthy, apparently, did not come to the same conclusion.

The interview with McCarthy was well done, despite a few flaws. The author treated his interview graciously and the interview is genuinely engaging. The interview primarily is designed to promote *The Road*, but McCarthy responded to Oprah's questions on a variety of topics. He gave new biographical details about his past and present. For example, he tells Oprah a story about how when he was in the early stages of his writing career, he was so poor that when a free sample of toothpaste arrived in the mail, it was like some kind of providential gift. In addition to sharing bits of trivia about his life, he also describes how he composed *The Road*, and he shares information about what he learned about writing while at the University of Tennessee.

The interview does contain a few awkward moments, particularly when she asks McCarthy about his depiction of women and his development of female characters. McCarthy responds to her inquiry by claiming that he does not understand women, at which point Oprah asks how that is possible after three marriages. The interview then quickly moves on without any substantial exploration of the issue.

In the interview, McCarthy articulates his sincere disdain for materialism. He also expresses his genuine disinterest in the number of people who read his books. While he treats the subject with humor, he clearly states that he does care whether or not people like his books. Oprah says that his lack of concern about book sales and numbers of readers differentiates him from other authors she knows.

Through the course of the interview, McCarthy provides some insight into the writing process that resulted in *The Road*. As part of this conversation, McCarthy makes the assertion that the subconscious is "older" than language. The context of this claim relates to how he composed *The Road*, which McCarthy compared to how some scientists achieve breakthroughs in their thinking. McCarthy posits that a complicated relationship exists between language and the unconscious. He also muses about consciousness—that is, being awake—as a state that may hinder the unconscious from communicating to the conscious mind. To develop this point, he recounts an episode about Henry Miller, who McCarthy says would sit in front of his typewriter and hold his hands above the keys while chanting "J'ecoute," which is French for "I am listening."

This desire for a mind uncluttered by language figures into his avoidance of the media. He claims that when writing a book, one should not be thinking or talking about other things, because by talking about books with other people (journalists, for example), he would somehow be altering the complex relationship between his conscious mind and his subconscious. His rejection of the media ensures that he will remain focused on his writing.

While a lot has been made of *The Road* in the United States, McCarthy does have a wide international audience. His work has been translated into French, German, and Italian, and his novels are particularly popular in France. He won the James Tait Black Award for *The Road*, which is the United Kingdom's most prestigious literary award and includes a prize of 10,000 pounds. McCarthy did not attend the ceremony. While McCarthy's work has been understood as quintessentially American, there is something transcendent about *The Road*. It seems to be reaching a wider audience than any of his other novels. There is also something uncanny about the book itself. Oprah said that as soon as she was done reading it, she wanted to read it again.

His novels interest a variety of luminaries, including Hollywood directors Joel and Ethan Coen. McCarthy's *Time* magazine interview with the Coen brothers only covers one page, but it is notable for its collegial nature, which the author is reportedly known for in his close circles. The interview reveals a side of McCarthy that is down-to-earth, not aloof or reclusive, and he is obviously a fan of the Coen brothers. This familiarity with their work suggests a more familiar relationship with popular culture than his works indicate.

On the heels of these more substantial interviews, McCarthy has become slightly more spontaneous on the issue of communicating with the media. The interview he granted to David Kushner of *Rolling Stone* in late 2007 was unplanned. Kushner was working on an article about *The Road*. As part of that piece, he was talking to theoretical physicist Lisa Randall, who is a member of the SFI where McCarthy is a fellow. As Kushner was talking with Randall, she said "let's go talk to Cormac." McCarthy obliged and also further accommodated the venture with a nice picture to introduce the article.

In Kushner's article, titled "Cormac McCarthy's Apocalypse," McCarthy covers much of the same subject matter that he does in the interview with Oprah. The primary difference here is that McCarthy talks extensively about the work conducted at the SFI and how the scientists in residence influenced the way he conceived of the apocalyptic world he depicts in *The Road*. Kushner's article adds to the growing popular interest in *The Road*, which continues to expand because of the anticipation about the forthcoming movie adaptation.

The movie rights to *The Road* were purchased by Chockstone Pictures immediately after the novel was released. For a book to win prizes in 2007 and then to have that book made into a feature movie by 2008 with a 2009 release date is an unusually accelerated time frame.

Although *The Road* enjoyed widespread popularity, the exact opposite was the case for *Blood Meridian*, the lukewarm popular reception of which has been well documented. *Time* magazine ranks McCarthy's 1985 masterpiece as one of the best 100 American novels since 1923. Although reception of the work by the general reading public continues to be uneven, academic circles regularly herald the text as a seminal masterpiece of American literature. Harold Bloom, a prominent critic at Yale University, lauds *Blood Meridian* as the best novel by any living American writer for its philosophical, historical, and aesthetic range.

The explosion in critical reviews of McCarthy's work following publication of *All the Pretty Horses* revealed the schism between the academic and popular reception of McCarthy's work. Reviewers, representing the voice of the general public, are almost always complimentary of McCarthy's prose; however, they tend to take a dim view of his cosmic pessimism. This pessimism does not seem to concern academics. In fact, the nihilistic qualities of his works have inspired critical acclaim and interest within academic circles. This split between popular reviewers and scholars reveals a fundamental difference of aesthetic opinion between reviewers and academics. McCarthy's academic supporters tend not to be critical of his pessimism, whereas many reviewers are not impressed with his bleak outlook on the current and future state of humanity.

This increase in public popularity created a demand for McCarthy scholars like Rick Wallach, presently the secretary of the Cormac McCarthy Society, to give public presentations about McCarthy. Wallach's understanding of McCarthy's audience is crucial for future readers of his work. Academics should not lose sight of the fact that the public at large likes interesting things to read, and that as high flown as a lot of McCarthy's work is, his novels cultivate a broad appeal.

While a small group of academics have written extensively about McCarthy's works, several reviews in popular media have helped make McCarthy's reputation more mainstream. Richard Woodward's articles in the *New York Times Book Review* and *Vanity Fair* are two primary examples. But one of the best reviews is Michael Chabon's review of *The*

Road, which appeared in the February 15, 2007, edition of the *New York Review of Books*. That particular novel received many reviews, but Chabon transcends the genre and provides a comprehensive commentary on McCarthy's entire body of work. Of particular interest is his claim that *The Road* is a work of horror, which Chabon defines as "stoicism with a taste for spectacle." While not a comprehensive explanation of the novel's power, Chabon's insight shows how McCarthy has not restricted his work to the conventions of any particular genre. In fact, McCarthy's writing is successful because he mixes genres with fascinating results.

McCarthy's use of the media can be categorized in two ways: he uses the media as a promotional tool for his fiction sparingly or not at all. However, his forays into teleplays, drama, and screenplay writing show an interest in using those media to reach as wide an audience as possible. Certainly, television and movie audiences would reach larger numbers than his readership. Consequently, the fact that he has sold five screenplays and that two of his novels (*Cities of the Plain* and *No Country for Old Men*) began as screenplays points to McCarthy's dual approach to using cinema as an outlet to promote his work. Furthermore, the extent of his attention to cinema indicates more than a passing interest.

At the same time that McCarthy's films have been increasing public awareness of his novels (even though there has been a mixed reception on the part of McCarthy's popular and academic reviewers), his reviews have also provided readers with a greater understanding of McCarthy's literary context. *The Road* ends with a curious image of a brook trout, an image that Oprah's Book Club discussed. Jennifer Egan, in a review of this novel for Slate.com, recalled the image as being reminiscent of Hemingway in his stories *Big Hearted River I and II*. There are two symbolic aspects to this image: McCarthy's pastoral impulse and his adoption of a Hemingway-esque style of writing in the latter stages of his career. McCarthy eschews Hemingway's ambiguity and some of his modernist style of repetition; however, he does employ a kind of minimalism and directness that is reminiscent of Hemingway.

From a thematic standpoint, the critical reception of *The Road* has been widely varied. In addition to Chabon's take on it as a quasi-horror novel and Egan's exploration of its connection to Hemingway, critics have seen in it apocalyptic biblical and environmental messages. Its father-son dynamic certainly lends itself to a biblical reading. Yet, a closer reading of the text proves that McCarthy is difficult to pin down on this issue, particularly when recalling the paradoxical statement of the father: "There is no God and we are his prophets" (p. 143).

What critics agree on is that the totally degraded environment is the dominant feature of the novel. The novel's popularity and uncompromising vision of total environmental destruction has caused one critic to say that this is the most important environmental novel ever written. The problem with such a statement is that it is unclear what caused the devastation—the circumstantial evidence points toward a nuclear war, but that is debatable. McCarthy's own statements made from his SFI office to *Rolling Stone*'s Kushner may clarify the novel. McCarthy says that humans will do themselves in before we destroy the environment to such a degree that it will no longer support us.

The debate about the environmental and religious implications of the book has yet to consider them simultaneously. Most reviewers interpret them as separate themes. What may get lost in the heavy subject matter of the novel and the critical responses to it is the fact that the novel contains a stern warning and has a powerful moral component. This morality further distances the novel from the generally fanciful tendencies of contemporary apocalyptic renderings which avoid how terrible a real apocalypse would be.

The media tends to emphasize the aesthetic experience of his works rather than the moral component. Morality, especially in his romantic works, tends to be occluded by the strength of the narratives, whereas in *The Road*, the morality and the narrative coexist comfortably. Consequently, the morality of his works is one thing that seems to be beyond the grasp of critics and even academics, to a degree. Critics have focused on aesthetics and academics have emphasized the historical and social aspects of his work and his place in the literary canon. McCarthy's moral constructs, in particular the ethical plights and decisions of his characters, evoke echoes of two of the oldest literary classics, Homer's epics, which will be discussed in the next chapter.

DISCUSSION QUESTIONS

- What do you think about the difference between the academic and popular reception of McCarthy's work?
- Why do you think McCarthy has allowed greater access to the media later in his career?
- Why do you think McCarthy gives greater access to popular media outlets rather than "serious" ones?
- How has Hollywood influenced popular reception of McCarthy's work?
- Do you think that McCarthy has given too much access to the popular media?

18

WHAT DO I READ NEXT?

McCarthy's unique prose tends to spoil his readers, making it difficult for devotees to move on to other writers. Whereas some authors tend to get readers engaged with certain kinds of subject matter, McCarthy's style and the voices of his fully realized characters can make other fiction a bit less palatable. Despite McCarthy's pessimism about humanity, and his admitted lack of concern for the numbers of his readers, he has spent his life trying to compose works that would provide his readers with a memorable aesthetic experience.

Based on his writing style, subject matter, and the content of his published interviews, some specific books and writers might interest readers of McCarthy's works. McCarthy's own intellectual interests are far ranging—his personal library allegedly contains more than seven thousand books. To mirror the scope of work that has influenced McCarthy's development as a writer, the following recommendations will be eclectic in that they cover a variety of areas, such as fiction, classical literature, philosophy, natural history, religious studies, and modern classics.

For those readers who enjoy the prose style of McCarthy's most recent novels, the novels and short stories of Ernest Hemingway are a good starting point. While some of Hemingway's modernist devices, particularly repetition, might seem dated, his directness, economy, and engaging narratives have aged well. Readers of McCarthy would find almost any Hemingway novel accessible; however, Hemingway is a master of the short story. Their clear dialogue and powerfully rendered characters immediately engage the reader, techniques that McCarthy employs in *The Road* and *No Country for Old Men*.

For readers interested in a fictional work that has clearly been influenced by McCarthy, Charles Frazier's novel *Cold Mountain* is worth reading. Set in the closing days of the Civil War in North Carolina, the novel echoes McCarthy's interest in Appalachian America and in simplistic rural settings that house weighty narratives. On the surface, the novel owes more to Homer's episodic structure of the *Odyssey*, but the book also features well-realized characters and tight narratives in the vein of McCarthy's style.

While Frazier's prose does not have the philosophical digressions that define much of McCarthy's prose, his prose does display a remarkable power of description of landscape and character. Frazier imbues his characters with tremendous pathos, and like McCarthy's fictional creations, these characters become ennobled by the futility and triumph of their various struggles. Frazier, like McCarthy, deftly handles the tragic ending; both authors are interested in the way that the world sunders ethical men and women from their desired destinies and from each other.

An interesting companion piece to Frazier is MacKinlay Kantor's book *Andersonville*. McCarthy speaks briefly about this book in his interview with Oprah. He cites this book as the influential source for not punctuating dialogue. Kantor's book has the same sort of relationship to historical matter that *Blood Meridian* does. Kantor bases his novel on historical characters using memoirs and first-hand interviews (Kantor spoke with Civil War veterans) to craft his narrative. Kantor's novel, like *Blood Meridian*, shows the possibilities that research can play in creating memorable fiction.

One novel that combines a striking command of language with unique subject matter is Katherine Dunn's comic masterpiece, *Geek Love*. It bears almost no resemblance to McCarthy's work; however, this particular novel can be seen as a comic treatment of the characters who appear in *Child of God* and *Outer Dark*. Dunn's novel is extremely anti-conformist and, because of its rebelliousness and high comedy, it has a well-deserved cult following. Dunn's novel explores the way in which a carnival family uses drugs and other techniques to produce freakish physical abnormalities in their offspring who then become the main attractions in the family's traveling show. Within the context of this narrative, Dunn's characters begin to implode amid a stew of human compulsions, such as jealousy, greed, and religious fervor.

Dunn, like McCarthy, has a slightly checkered past in which she existed on society's periphery. Her own picaresque adventures include blowing advances for novels to run off to Ireland with her boyfriend and landing in jail for passing bad checks. She also supported herself by writing about boxing. Her interest in boxing stems from its unusual place in current American culture as a sport that is still highly individualistic and violent. Those two elements characterize much of *Geek Love*. Her biography is similar to McCarthy's in that she is a consummate outsider, who has brought a powerful story into mainstream literary culture. Dunn's popularity belies the fact that many people identify with outsiders, rejects, castoffs, freaks, and so on.

Dunn has said in interviews that at the time she was writing the book, she was concerned about the hyperconformity that defined American society in the late 1980s and early 1990s. The cultural evolution of the twenty-first century has probably added to her anxiety as vocalized by the many scholars, parents, and culture critics who decry the ways in which the technological culture is producing a mind-numbing sameness of character. One antidote to this technological saturation is reading powerfully imagined fiction. Dunn's energetic novel has that intangible quality that, like much of McCarthy's work, is paradoxically moral and decadent.

Another cult favorite that would be of interest to McCarthy readers who admire sublime prose is John Kennedy Toole's *A Confederacy of Dunces*. Toole's novel, published posthumously after the author's suicide, is a modern classic. The book might best be described as a comic *Suttree*, with its epic scope, cast of characters, and a disdainful and loathsome protagonist. Both novels are set in specific places—New Orleans (Toole) and Knoxville (McCarthy)—and owe the energy of these settings to distinctive places in the South. Both novels examine characters who inhabit the margins of society. Toole's protagonist, Ignatius Reilly, cultivates feelings of both empathy and disgust from readers but with a comic touch that is lacking in all of McCarthy's Southern gothic works. Toole's vividly rendered characters give this comic epic lasting power.

Another novel that blends virtuosity of prose with compelling subject matter is Toni Morrison's *Beloved*. McCarthy and Morrison share some authorial common ground. Like McCarthy, Morrison is fascinated with American history, and this novel in particular finds its impetus in an historic occurrence, which is similar to McCarthy's masterpiece, *Blood Meridian*. Both books appear regularly on lists that rank the best American novels, such as those by *Time* magazine and the *New York Review of Books*. Of greater interest is both authors' complex treatment of race and poverty in America. Both McCarthy and Morrison create morally complex characters from people who are barely literate or who are completely illiterate. Both write movingly about what it is like to be poor in America. Both valorize the struggle of humans to survive, which reveals an element of classicism in their work. They see common elements in humanity, which underlie the uniqueness of each individual's life.

Struggle is inherent to the human condition and the exploration of that theme is essential for great fiction. McCarthy's classical approach to this theme stems from two major sources, Homer and the German philosopher Friedrich Nietzsche. Reading the epics of Homer will make McCarthy's work more accessible, but most important, these ancient works are as relevant today as they were when they were created. They represent a continuity of the human experience that transcends time. The epic that renders this struggle most effectively is Homer's *Odyssey*; however, it is the tragic worldview depicted in the *Iliad* that is most clearly reflected in McCarthy's work. The second section of McCarthy's novel *The Crossing* opens with the sentence: "Doomed enterprises forever divide lives into the then and the now" (p. 129). To understand why some of McCarthy's male protagonists seem to embrace futile or lost causes, it is essential to reference the *Iliad*, and especially, its doomed young male warrior, Achilles. Homer's richly imagined and gifted hero is timeless because of his rebellious romantic tendencies. Achilles holds himself to a strict code of idiosyncratic ethics that will not be influenced by any outside forces. Achilles' emotionalism is also of interest in its stark contrast to the stoicism of McCarthy's characters. What is most interesting, however, is that Achilles is angry because he knows he is doomed. This overwhelming predestination imbues the epic with energy, especially in the way that Achilles ultimately embraces his destiny.

While Homer's epic hardly needs another endorsement for its readability or contemporary relevance, its connection to McCarthy is important because it represents a kind of archetypal continuity. The nobility of Achilles' character is seen in many of McCarthy's characters, male and female, throughout his novels and plays. Achilles' doomed nature and how he faces his destiny ennobles him and his struggle. Thus, the archetype, the originating pattern, which McCarthy takes from Homer, is how the world destroys "ethical" or noble people.

However, ethical and noble do not necessarily mean good. This philosophical ambiguity is a crucial idea that McCarthy culls from Nietzsche. Before exploring Nietzsche's idea of morality, it is important to discuss the ways in which the *Odyssey* redeems the tragic nature of human existence as it pertains to nobility in the *Iliad*.

The *Odyssey* contains the character of Odysseus, who serves as the archetype for many McCarthy characters. Odysseus' wanderings, in which he displays tremendous resourcefulness, provides the foundation for many of McCarthy's narratives and characters. McCarthy's male characters embrace adventure and uncertain futures in a heroic manner—this is evinced by "good' characters, such as John Grady Cole in *All the Pretty Horses,* and with ignoble characters, such as the kid in *Blood Meridian.* Thus, what links the *Odyssey* to McCarthy is a strain of epic individualism in which his characters are both defeated by the world and society and in which the world and society defeat the same types of noble characters. What further links his narratives to Homer is that his characters develop their intellect and their bodies through the course of these narratives. This reflects the classical ideal of "a sound mind in a sound body."

The emphasis on physicality and intellectualism in a context of complete individualism and autonomy—which, in Homer, is represented by Achilles' complete rejection of the Greeks' pleas to join the fight outside Troy and by Odysseus' total solitude in the latter half of the *Odyssey*—finds its representational counterparts in almost all works by McCarthy. This type of heroic individualism might seem anachronistic to modern audiences, but it is all the more relevant in the early twenty-first century's mass culture in which individuals are in constant contact and rely heavily on one another for survival. The relationship between Homer's epics and McCarthy's novels may represent a kind of nostalgia, but they do not do so in the sentimental sense, that is, not in the sense of yearning for a bygone era, but rather in a productive sense in which these ideals should not be forgotten.

To understand and to appreciate McCarthy's incorporation of historical material into his fiction, consider several works of nonfiction. The first is an important work of cultural history, *Of Wolves and Men* by Barry Lopez. This book was discussed earlier in relation to *The Crossing.* Lopez's work supplies important contextual information for understanding McCarthy's writing about wolves; but its thorough research, engaging prose, and philosophical stance make it a classic worth reading in its own right. Lopez's intellectual and philosophical approach to the history of wolves in Europe and the United States has much to offer to a variety of readers. His interviews of wolf trappers and his attention to Native Americans and their relationship to wolves present a unique and complex analysis of the wolf as both symbol and animal. Drawing on science, philosophy, literature, folklore, and natural history, Lopez's book is thematically far ranging like many of McCarthy's novels and feeds both intellect and imagination.

Lopez's position as an intellectual outside of the academy—he does not hold any specific academic position, although he has helped design and contribute to an interdisciplinary program at Texas Tech—bears comparison with McCarthy. Lopez is independent, somewhat reclusive, something of a polymath, and was, like McCarthy, brought up Catholic. Lopez's religious background is not apparent in this book, but, like, McCarthy, a powerful sense of ethics permeates all of his writing. Lopez has a rich body of work, including a collection called *Crossing Open Ground,* which contains several essays that function as companion pieces to *Of Wolves and Men.*

Having just mentioned Cormac McCarthy's Catholicism, now would be an appropriate time to make a couple of recommendations about the nexus of religion and philosophy in McCarthy's work. This profound metaphysical intersection is one of the things that have inspired so many academics to be interested in his work. While there are many appropriate recommendations to make, several make for good starting points for ambitious readers. The first is Elaine Pagels's book *The Gnostic Gospels,* a work of religious history. In addition to Pagels's work, there are the Gnostic Gospels themselves, a good edition of which is published under the title, *The Nag Hammadi Library.* These gospels were excluded from the New Testament; however, they make for interesting historical reading. McCarthy's earlier works from his first novel up through *Blood Meridian* reveal some Gnostic sensibilities. Leo Daugherty has written a powerful essay about Gnosticism in *Blood Meridian;* however, that essay is more meaningful after first reading Pagels's book. Some of Pagels's book tells the story of how early Christianity was able to take such a powerful hold over ancient Roman society. One of the most engaging sections describes how early Christians identified with the suffering of Jesus as a human and not as the son of God. This idea of the redemption of human suffering is crucial to McCarthy's work. Of equal importance in McCarthy's work is the idea of human suffering without redemption—an idea that has its roots in two books by Nietzsche, *The Genealogy of Morals* and *The Birth of Tragedy.*

Nietzsche's ideas on tragedy and morality figure prominently in the works of McCarthy. McCarthy, like Nietzsche, perceives morality as a means by which the callow masses can sometimes control the strong-willed individual. In such a world, the strong-willed individual has two destinies, death or victory. McCarthy's strong-willed characters usually die. This tragic worldview stems from Nietzsche's treatise, *The Birth of Tragedy.* Nietzsche sees tragedy as the highest point of existence because he believes that suffering, whether redeemed or not, is the point at which humans are "most alive."

This worldview is explored by McCarthy throughout his work. Nietzsche comes to these conclusions by reading Greek tragedies; in fact, Nietzsche claims that all modern Western cultures after the Greeks grub around in the past looking for something to hang onto because their own societies are so shallow. Thus, in Greek tragedy, Nietzsche sees humanity in its most ennobled form. He absorbs much from Aristotle's observation that human beings empathize with a tragic character because they are better than us. This idea that someone is better than someone else is certainly antithetical to much modern thinking, particularly in the egalitarian and democratic society pervasive in the twenty-first century. It is crucial, however, not to confuse the idea of individual superiority with equality. McCarthy and Nietzsche embrace a heroic quality of the soul that cannot be destroyed or be made to conform. Simply stated, both men write about an inherent human greatness.

In addition to classical philosophy and tragedies, two modern classic authors are frequently invoked in discussions about McCarthy's influences: Herman Melville and William Faulkner. *Blood Meridian* reprises many essential qualities and themes of Melville's masterpiece, *Moby Dick*. Ahab's mania, Ishmael's metaphysical quest, the book's encyclopedic and epic scope, the questioning of American ideals, and the nature of racism are all crucial ingredients from Melville that McCarthy employs. The main distinction between the two authors is that McCarthy is writing historical fiction and Melville wrote in and of his particular time. That difference of historical representation shows how McCarthy places himself within a particular tradition of the American novel. In addition to viewing McCarthy as the heir to Melville's tradition, *Moby Dick* and *Blood Meridian* function as powerful companion pieces. For example, McCarthy's judge—bald, hairless, and nearly albino—is the sometimes-human equivalent of Melville's white whale.

It might seem natural to read *Moby Dick* before *Blood Meridian*, but Melville's novel can also be understood in retrospect after a careful reading of McCarthy. Melville's prose, which at first blush seems antiquated and Victorian, seems much more modern after reading McCarthy. Also, Melville's digressions into the etymological and natural history of whales, as well as the aesthetic, religious, and philosophical chapters, seem less tedious and more essential to an unconventional construction of the narrative tension after reading *Blood Meridian*.

The second modern classic that readers of McCarthy should consider exploring is William Faulkner's *Absalom, Absalom!* McCarthy has been compared to Faulkner more than any other writer, so any of Faulkner's novels would hold interest for students of McCarthy's work. To get a sense of the source of McCarthy's interest in the fall of the South, Faulkner's novel provides what might be the most poignant portrayal of that theme. Faulkner's novel contains the violence, the desire for a pastoral existence, the trope of the imbecile, and the nostalgia for the past that are hallmarks of McCarthy's Southern gothic novels. Yet, Faulkner's novel is different from McCarthy's work in that it explores race in ways that McCarthy does not. The novel is also a mystery, albeit an unconventional one. Finally, Faulkner's astounding blend of formal prose, dialect, and philosophical digressions clearly influenced McCarthy. Yet, by the time McCarthy was writing his Western or postapocalyptic novels, he had shed the influence of his towering predecessor and developed his own style.

One final recommendation should be considered by readers of McCarthy, and it is one of genre. McCarthy's novel *No Country for Old Men* takes its title from William Butler Yeats's poem "Sailing to Byzantium." All of McCarthy's novels are rife with prose that is highly lyrical and imagistic, suggesting the author has a familiarity with poetry as a form. McCarthy's prose evokes poetic structure in that both tend to distill important moments into a few words that are remarkably vivid and memorable. Many passages in *Suttree*, for example, reflect these poetic sensibilities, particularly when the protagonist wanders off into the Smoky Mountains.

Poetry requires that readers slow down both mind and eye, because poetry is not designed to be read quickly or silently. The fact that poetry is better read aloud is a testament to its origins in song. The form has evolved greatly over time; for example, classic poetry tends to use rhyme whereas modern poetry does not. By becoming attuned to these and other nuances of poetry, readers will have an additional tool with which to develop an understanding of and appreciation for some of the more intentional aspects of the construction of McCarthy's prose that otherwise might be subsumed within his engaging narratives.

This is a brief and wildly incomplete list, yet the works here will reward readers' close attention. Perhaps most important, when considering the author's works, readers should sustain the mental image of McCarthy reading, voraciously and alone, in his barracks in Alaska during the late 1950s. It was during this time that McCarthy seriously engaged the practice of reading and used those novels to mold himself into the artist and man he is today.

RESOURCES

Ambrosiano, Jason. "Blood in the Tracks: Catholic Postmodernism in *The Crossing.*" *Southwestern American Literature* 25, no. 1 (1999).

Arnold, Edwin T. "Introduction." *The Cormac McCarthy Journal* 4 (2005): 2–6.

Arnold, Edwin T. and Dianne C. Luce, eds. *A Cormac McCarthy Companion.* Jackson: University Press of Mississippi, 2001.

Bell, James. *Cormac McCarthy's West: The Border Trilogy Annotations.* El Paso: Texas Western, 2002.

Bloom, Harold, ed. *Cormac McCarthy.* Philadelphia: Chelsea House, 2002.

Bowles, Scott. "New Film Is in Coen Brothers 'Country.'" *USA Today,* November 8, 2007, 1D.

Breznican, Anthony. "Oscars in the Wings: Nerves, Tears and Cheers Just Off-stage." *USA Today,* February 25, 2008. http://www.usatoday.com/life/movies/movieawards/oscars/2008-02-25-oscars-cover_N.htm (accessed February 27, 2008).

Chabon, Michael. "After the Apocalypse." *The New York Review of Books* 54, no. 2 (2007). http://www.nybooks.com/articles/19856 (accessed December 8, 2007).

Chollier, Christine, ed. *Cormac McCarthy: Uncharted Territories/Territoires Inconnus.* Reims, France: Presses Universitaires de Reims, 2003.

Ciuba, Gary M. *Desire Violence & Divinity in Modern Southern Fiction.* Baton Rouge: Louisiana State University Press, 2007.

Cremean, David. "For Whom the Bell Tolls: Conservatism and Change in Cormac McCarthy's Sheriff from *No Country for Old Men.*" *The Cormac McCarthy Journal* 5 (2005): 21–29.

Cunningham, Mark Allen. "The Art of Reading Cormac McCarthy." *Poets and Writers,* September–October 2007.

Daugherty, Leo. "Gravers False and True: *Blood Meridian* as Gnostic Tragedy." In *Perspectives on Cormac McCarthy*, edited by Edwin T. Arnold and Dianne C. Luce. Jackson: University Press of Mississippi, 1999.

Duralde, Alonso. "Oscar Will Love 'No Country for Old Men.'" MSNBC.com, February 19, 2008. http://www.msnbc.msn.com/id/23239319/print/1/displaymode/1098/ (accessed February 21, 2008).

Egan, Jennifer. "Men at Work." Slate.com, October 10, 2006. http://www.slate.com/id/2151300/ (accessed May 8, 2008).

Eitzen, Stanley D. and Maxine Baca Zinn. *In Conflict and Order: Understanding Society.* 6th ed. Boston: Allyn and Bacon, 1993.

Ellis, Jay. *No Place for Home: Spatial Constraint and Character Flight in the Novels of Cormac McCarthy.* Edited by William E. Cain. New York: Routledge, 2006.

Germain, David. "Coen Brothers' Film 'No Country' Grabs Screen Actors' Awards." *The Plain Dealer,* January 28, 2008, D3.

Gibson, Mike. "'He Felt at Home in This Place': Knoxville Gave Cormac McCarthy the Raw Material of His Art. And He Gave It Back." *Metro Pulse*, Knoxville, TN. March, 1, 2001: 10–14, 16.

Grossman, Lev. "A Conversation between Cormac McCarthy and Joel and Ethan Coen about the New Movie *No Country for Old Men*." *Time,* October 29, 2007.

Guillemin, Georg. *The Pastoral Vision of Cormac McCarthy.* Edited by William T. Pilkington. College Station: Texas A&M University Press, 2004.

Guinn, Matthew. *After Southern Modernism.* Jackson: University Press of Mississippi, 2000.

Hall, Wade, and Rick Wallach, eds. *Sacred Violence: A Reader's Companion to Cormac McCarthy.* El Paso: Texas Western, 1995.

———, eds. *Sacred Violence.* 2nd ed., 2 vols. El Paso: Texas Western, 2002.

Holloway, David. *The Late Modernism of Cormac McCarthy.* Westport, CT: Greenwood, 2002.

———, ed. *Polemics: Essays in American Literary & Cultural Criticism.* Sheffield, UK: Black Rock, 2004.

Hooper, Ernest. "Prom Night, Valentine Delight." *St. Petersburg Times,* February 13, 2002. http://www.sptimes.com/2002/02/13/Columns/Prom_night_valentine.shtml (access February 28, 2008).

Jaynes, Gregory. "The Knock at the Door." Time.com, June 6, 1994. http://www.time.com/time/printout/0,8816,980861,00.html (accessed December 25, 2007).

Kakutani, Michiko. "On the Loose in Badlands: Killer with a Cattle Gun." *New York Times,* July 18, 2005. http://www.nytimes.com/2005/07/18/books/18kaku.html?scp=1&sq=&st=nyt (accessed April 23, 2009).

Kristof, Nicholas D. "No Conspiracy Theory Explains American Dumbness." *The Plain Dealer,* April 1, 2008, B7.

Kushner, David. "Cormac McCarthy's Apocalypse." *Rolling Stone,* December 27, 2007.

Lane, Anthony. "Hunting Grounds." *The New Yorker,* November 12, 2007.

Lilley, James D., ed. *Cormac McCarthy.* Albuquerque: University of New Mexico Press, 2002.

Lopez, Barry. *Crossing Open Ground.* New York: Vintage Books, 1989.

———. *Of Wolves and Men.* New York: Simon and Schuster, 1978.

McCarthy, Cormac. *All the Pretty Horses.* New York: Vintage International, 1993.

———. *Blood Meridian.* New York: Vintage International, 1992.

———. *Child of God.* New York: Vintage International, 1993.

———. *Cities of the Plain.* New York: Alfred A. Knopf, 1998.

———. *Crossing, The.* New York: Vintage International, 1995.

———. *Gardener's Son, The.* Hopewell, NJ: Ecco Press, 1996.

———. *No Country for Old Men.* New York: Alfred A. Knopf, 2005.

———. *Orchard Keeper, The.* New York: Vintage International, 1993.

———. *Outer Dark.* New York: Vintage International, 1993.

———. *Road, The.* New York: Alfred A. Knopf, 2006.

———. *Stonemason, The.* New York: Vintage International, 1995.

———. *Sunset Limited, The.* New York: Vintage International, 2006.

———. *Suttree.* New York: Vintage International, 1992.

McGrath, Charles. "At World's End, Honing a Father-Son Dynamic." *New York Times,* May 27, 2008. http://www.nytimes.com/2008/05/27/movies/27road.html?_r=2&oref=slogin&oref=slogin.htm (accessed May 31, 2008).

Miller, Danny L., Sharon Hatfield, and Gurney Norman, eds. *An American Vein.* Athens: Ohio University Press, 2005.

Morrow, Mark. *Images of the Southern Writer.* Athens: University of Georgia Press, 1985.

Owens, Barclay. *Cormac McCarthy's Western Novels.* Tucson: University of Arizona Press, 2000.

Payne, Roger. *Among Whales.* New York: Scribner, 1995.

Rothfork, John. "Cormac McCarthy as Pragmatist." *Critique: Studies in Contemporary Fiction* 47, no. 2 (2006).

Sanborn, Wallis R., III. *Animals in the Fiction of Cormac McCarthy.* Jefferson, NC: McFarland & Company, 2006.

Schimpf, Shane. *A Reader's Guide to Blood Meridian.* Seattle, WA: Bon Mot Publishing, 2006.

Sepich, John. *Notes on Blood Meridian.* Austin: University of Texas Press, 2008.

Seton, Ernest Thompson. *Wild Animals I Have Known*. Toronto: McClelland & Stewart, 1898.

Sheppard, R.Z. "Thar She Moos." Time.com, May 18, 1998. http://www.time.com/time/printout/0,8816,988357,00.html (accessed December 25, 2007).

Spillman, Rob. "Book of Revelation." Bookforum.com, December 2007. http://www.bookforum.com/archive/dec_06/spillman.html (accessed February 6, 2008).

Tatum, Stephen. *Cormac McCarthy's* All the Pretty Horses. New York: Continuum, 2002.

The Editors. "Up Front." *New York Times,* July 24, 2005. http://www.nytimes.com/2005/07/24/books/review/24UPFRONT.html?_r=2&oref=slogin (accessed May 8, 2008).

Vancheri, Barbara. "Filming of 'The Road' Leads to Pittsburgh." *Pittsburgh Post-Gazette,* January 16, 2008. http://www.postgazette.com/pg/08016/849427-42.stm (accessed January 17, 2008).

Wallace, Garry. "Meeting McCarthy." *Southern Quarterly* (Summer 1992).

Wallach, Rick, ed. *Myth, Legend, Dust: Critical Responses to Cormac McCarthy.* Manchester, UK: Manchester University Press, 2000.

Warner, Alan. "The Road to Hell." *Guardian,* November 4, 2006. http://www.guardian.co.uk/books/2006/nov/04/featuresreviews.guardianreview4 (accessed May 7, 2008).

Williams, Don. "All the Pretty Colors of Cormac McCarthy (Has the Master of the Macabre Gone Soft?)." *The Chattahoochee Review* 13, no. 4 (1993): 1–7.

———. "Annie DeLisle: Cormac McCarthy's Ex-Wife Prefers to Recall the Romance." *The Knoxville News Sentinel,* June 10, 1990, E1.

———. "Cormac McCarthy: Knoxville's Most Famous Contemporary Writer Prefers His Anonymity." *The Knoxville News Sentinel,* June 10, 1990, E1.

Winchell, Mark Royden. *Reinventing the South.* Columbia: University of Missouri Press, 2006.

Wood, James. "Notes from Underground." *The New Yorker,* March 2008.

———. "Red Planet: The Sanguinary Sublime of Cormac McCarthy." Newyorker.com, July 25, 2005. http://www.newyorker.com/archive/2005/07/25/050725crbo_books?printable=true (accessed January 17, 2008).

Woodward, Richard B. "Cormac Country." *Vanity Fair,* August 2005.

———. "Cormac McCarthy's Venomous Fiction." *New York Times Book Review,* April 19, 1992. http://query.nytimes.com/gst/fullpage.html?res=9E0CE6DA163EF93AA25757C0A964958260 (accessed March 8, 2009).

INDEX

About the Author

WILLARD P. GREENWOOD is associate professor of English and chair of the English Department at Hiram College. He is the editor-in-chief of the *Hiram Poetry Review*, and his writing has appeared in such outlets as *Yale Angler's Journal, Passages North*, and *American Literary Review*.